Creative Ice Skating

Ice Dancing, Freestyle, and Pair Skating

Frances Dorsey and Wendy Williams

Contemporary Books, Inc.
Chicago

Library of Congress Cataloging in Publication Data

Dorsey, Frances.
    Creative ice skating.

    Includes index.
    1. Skating.   I. Williams, Wendy, joint author.
II. Title.
GV850.4.D67   1980   796.91   80-65923
ISBN 0-8092-7107-9
ISBN 0-8092-7106-0 (pbk.)

Published by Contemporary Books, Inc.
180 North Michigan Avenue, Chicago, Illinois 60601
Manufactured in the United States of America
Library of Congress Catalog Card Number: 80-65923
International Standard Book Number: 0-8092-7107-9 (cloth)
                                    0-8092-7106-0 (paper)

Published simultaneously in Canada by
Beaverbooks
953 Dillingham Road
Pickering, Ontario L1W 1Z7
Canada

Contents

Acknowledgments

Photo credit to Joseph Van Zandt for skating shots taken at the Northbrook Sports Complex, Northbrook, Illinois. Additional chapter opening photos courtesy of Steve White and Larry Miller. Cover photo credit to Robert Meyers.

Many thanks to Joseph Van Zandt for his valuable technical advice. And to Cal James and Dorsey Plummer, who both appear with Ms. Dorsey in the pictures throughout the book.

A special thanks is extended to Dick Friesen for his musical knowledge and advice.

Introduction

The house lights slowly dim and a hush settles over the audience. The orchestra strikes up a sunny overture and the rink lights burst into color. Scores of gaily costumed skaters enter for the opening number. The tempo of the music and the skating gradually increase in a crescendo of sound and color until a high point is reached.

Suddenly, the lights go black and a single spotlight picks you up as you make your grand entrance to the cheers of the audience. In a blur of speed and a flurry of dazzling moves, you flash across the ice, performing spectacular leaps and spins that elicit oohs and aahs from the crowd.

Two hours later, the show comes to a rousing, spectacular finish, and you and your company of skaters are brought back for encore after encore.

Far-fetched? Not on your life. After all, where do you think those glamorous skaters all come from? Most come from ordinary backgrounds. They learned to skate on a farm pond, a frozen river, or perhaps a rink of a city playground. They got where they are because their love of skating gave them the desire, the will, and the stamina to put in long hours, day after day, year after year, until they were among the best skaters in the world.

Of course, most of us who skate don't wish to make the kind of major commitment that it takes to become a top amateur skater or a professional entertainer, but that doesn't have to spell the end of our relationship with the sport of skating. Literally thousands of people across the country belong to skating clubs, race in all types of events, belong to local hockey leagues, or simply skate with family and friends for the sheer fun of it.

The purpose of this book is to introduce you, the skater, to the fascinating world of figure skating. You may find, after learning how complex it is that you may not want to become a full-time skating enthusiast or student. Fine— now you'll have a few new tricks in your bag for impressing family and friends. And you just

Fran Dorsey executing a maneuver she invented "The Dorsey."

might discover, after trying and mastering a few basic turns and jumps, that ice-skating has you on the hook.

The story of Frances Dorsey is a case in point. At the tender age of six, during a family vacation to Sun Valley, Idaho—a resort known at one time as much for its skating as its skiing—she laced up a pair of skates for the first time. Like so many young girls in the 1940s, she watched the movies that starred the beautiful and glamorous Sonja Henie, and then spent countless hours on the ice practicing and pretending that she was a famous ice-skating star.

Fran joined a local skating club and got her first real taste of figure-skating competition and ice-show performing. By the time she was ten, she had won the Juvenile Pacific Coast Championship, the first of a long string of honors in her career. Later she won the National Junior Ladies title and was selected for the U.S. Olympic and World teams.

At eighteen, Fran was offered a leading role in the Ice Follies; so she turned professional. During her five years with the show, she took dancing lessons and strove to improve the performing side of her skating abilities. During this time she was a lead in Holiday on Ice. When she married and began to raise a family, she remained devoted to skating by using her skills to teach others. For eight of the past twelve years, Fran has been "head pro" at the Northbrook, Illinois, Sports Complex, which has the largest skating school in the country—1,500 students. And for eleven of the twelve years, she has choreographed the complex's annual ice show, which includes more than 1,000 participants.

At one point in her career, Fran was invited to skate in a Las Vegas ice show at Caesar's

Palace. While there she met her present husband, Dick Friesen, who was musical director for the revue. They joined forces to form their own ice show, America on Ice, through which Fran has pursued her ideas about theater on ice and has turned ice-skating into a true art form. She has also skated throughout the country and world including performances at Knott's Berry Farm; Sea World (Orlando); the Sahara Taho (Lake Taho); Drury Lane Theater (Chicago); and a 16-month cultural exchange in Taiwan.

Ice-skating may not become as big a part of your life as it has of Fran's, but her immeasurable talent and experience will surely benefit you no matter what your skating objectives are. And once you have tried the moves she describes, and have gone through the routines she outlines, you, too, seek stardom on ice.

PHOTOGRAPHY BY
Steve White

1
History of Skating

Ice-skating is one of the world's oldest sports. It can be traced back nearly 3,000 years to the Stone Age in northern Europe. In its early form, it was a means of transportation. Bone runners, fashioned from the ribs of elk and reindeer, were strapped onto the bottoms of boots. Early skaters ground the bones down to make a flat surface for better gliding. The oldest existing skates, discovered bound to the feet of a prehistoric man in Holland, were made from the bones of a horse. A spiked staff, much like a ski pole, was used to propel a skater across the ice. Since skating was a serious means of travel, anything that helped develop speed was desirable.

During the Middle Ages, skating was common on the frozen Dutch canals in winter. A fifteenth-century Dutch woodcut depicts a young girl collapsed on the ice among her friends. As legend has it, she broke her rib while skating and, failing to recover, spent the rest of her life in a religious order. The girl later became known as St. Lydwina, the patron saint of skaters.

At about the same time as St. Lydwina's accident, speed skating began to develop in Holland. The interwoven Dutch canals were ideal for speed, and Dutch skaters perfected the sport on the ice networks. Bone skates were replaced by wooden skates that were easier to carve and shape, and in the mid-1500s a wood and metal combination evolved. The first all-metal skate was supposedly developed in Russia in the late 1600s.

The Dutch are even said to have won a battle or two on skates, by outwitting their Spanish enemies during a winter siege. An icebound Spanish ship and freezing cargo were no match for experienced Dutch skaters. Hockey is said to have begun with these "ice fights."

The first skating club was formed in Edinburgh, Scotland, in 1742; and in France, Marie Antoinette skated in Paris with the French aristocracy, which eagerly took to the sport in the late 1700s. As a boy, Napoleon almost drowned when he fell through the ice that covered the moat around the fort at Auxerre.

In 1850, E. W. Bushnell invented the first all-steel skate. It clipped to the boot bottom, eliminating the time-consuming use of straps.

America developed a love of the sport, too; and skating clubs and private skating rinks began to appear. A skating rink on the lake in New York's Central Park was a sensation, and in 1862 a winter carnival was organized on Union Pond in Brooklyn. Six years later, the first skating rink in Canada was opened in Toronto. But it was a man from Chicago, Jackson Haines, who revolutionized the sport. He introduced ballroom dancing techniques to skating and won an American championship in New York.

In 1864 Haines went to Europe and his techniques overwhelmed the conventional European ways of skating. He helped to form the Viennese school of skating and to develop international style regulations.

Skating thrived in Scandinavia, too. Alex Paulsen of Norway was a force in Scandinavian skating, and Ulrich Salchow of Sweden won the world championship ten times. Their names are still connected with types of skating jumps. Many others followed, such as Gilles Grafstrom and Sonja Henie.

The first indoor ice rink was opened in London in 1876, and the next year saw a proliferation of rinks on both sides of the ocean—in Belgium, France, and Germany, and in American cities such as Baltimore, New York, and Philadelphia.

The International Skating Union (ISU) was formed in Davos, Switzerland, in 1892, and today it has thirty-two member-nations. The ISU supervises all forms of skating, including speed skating, figure skating, and ice dancing. Figure skating was recognized in the Olympics in 1908.

Lake Placid, New York, hosted the Winter Olympics in 1932, and after those games the popularity of Sonja Henie, who won the women's figure-skating gold medal, focused attention on the sport. Her blond Norwegian hair and lithe figure captured the hearts of the world. Besides doing professional ice shows, Sonja starred in Hollywood films like *Sun Valley Serenade*. Her personal appearances and acting brought skating to the attention of the world and made Miss Henie a millionaire.

With its flash and glamour, figure skating has always been more popular than speed skating. Both Anne Henning and Diane Holum, who were trained in Northbrook, Illinois, won gold medals in speed skating, but neither was ever offered a position in an ice show.

While European speed skaters have many Olympic-size rinks to practice on, American skaters have only two—one in West Allis, Wisconsin, and the other, newly opened, in Lake Placid, New York. The rink at Squaw Valley, California, was closed after its use for the 1960 Winter Olympics.

Today, smaller indoor ice rinks have sprung up all over, with major metropolitan cities many times having more rinks than skaters to support them. Rinks now have programs that appeal to all types of skaters, whether they are practicing professionals or recreational skaters.

Professional ice-skating shows now draw large audiences to watch the skilled routines of skaters wearing spectacular costumes. These shows not only have unique choreography that mixes elements of drama with intricate moves, but touches of humor, as well. Top-name skating celebrities, such as Dorothy Hamill, Peggy Fleming, and Fran Dorsey, continue to win the hearts of today's skaters.

Equipment

BUY OR RENT?

Skates are the first major investment that anyone seriously interested in skating will make. If you are only going to skate once or twice, renting skates is a good idea. But rental skates have disadvantages—hundreds of pairs of feet have stretched and broken them down. Wearing rental skates is at times no better than wearing a pair of mittens. With skates that give no support to the ankle, it's no wonder that beginning skaters complain of having "weak ankles." This malady could be entirely avoided with properly fitting boots and blades. There simply isn't a medical disability known as "weak ankles."

Anyone skating at least once a week will save money and learn to skate much easier and faster by buying his own skates. Not only are you guaranteed a better fitting boot, with excellent support, but also you are assured of having the blade that best suits your type of skating.

Different blades are used for compulsory figures, jumps, spins, and ice dancing. Most beginning figure skaters use an all-purpose skate with a blade approximately ⅛-inch wide. It is hollow ground so that only the two outer edges of the blade touch the ice while you are standing. The toepicks are uniform, not as prominent or jagged as those used for jumping.

The boot, or shoe, should be constructed of firm leather and fit snugly when laced. Skate sizes are usually smaller (generally anywhere from one-half to one full size smaller) than a normal walking shoe. For instance, if you take a 7B shoe, you would purchase a 6 or 6½B ice skate.

But never sacrifice quality in order to save money. A boot that has cheap, floppy leather or a poor blade that slides as easily sideways as it does forward will only hinder your skating. You won't be able to learn easily, and the cost of lessons and equipment will soon be lost, as interest starts to wane from lack of progress. A good pair of skates is well worth the initial investment and will last a long time if well taken care of after each use.

THE BOOT

A good quality leather boot will not lose its shape after a couple of months of wear. A good boot should fit snugly, not tightly, and comfortably at the ankle and throughout the foot. Up and down movement in the heel means that you probably need a boot a size smaller. And when you bend your knees, there shouldn't be too much buckling of the leather around the ankle. While a larger boot might feel more comfortable at first, the boot that fits snugly is a better choice. After a few sessions of skating to break the boot in, it will conform to your foot.

Choose a boot that has a built-in arch support, or counter, that is either of strong leather or steel. The tongue of the boot should be well lined, too.

When trying on skates, wear only a thin sock or a pair of tights. A thick heavy sock will reduce the support qualities of the boot. A common fallacy is the notion that thick socks keep your feet warmer—they don't. A thick sock can actually make your foot feel colder because you have to lace the boot tightly to get the support that you need; this cuts off circulation and makes your feet cold.

THE BLADE

Always make sure that the blade of the skate is quality steel. This will assure good gliding qualities and the ability to sharpen the blade properly.

The toepicks should not hinder the skater. Although correct pushes are made from the side of the blade—not from the toe—the toepicks help the beginner because, when the pushing foot is turned out, the lowest pick leaves the ice last and prevents the blade from slipping sideways.

If you find that you are tripping over your toepick, it is because the foot is being used incorrectly. If the lowest toepicks are very sharp, you will get used to them—don't have them ground off. Once the picks are gone, they can't be replaced.

The bottom of the blade of the skate is hollow, permitting an edge on each side—an outside edge and an inside edge—to touch the ice.

If the hollow isn't there, the blade will slide sideways and make pushing impossible. Professional sharpeners know how to sharpen the skates correctly to restore the hollow.

The depth of the hollow is important, too. Too deep a hollow will cause the blade to sink too far into the ice, making the skate difficult to maneuver, and too shallow a hollow results in skidding and loss of edge. Depending on what type of skating you will be doing, it is best to consult a professional about the depth of the hollow needed.

Many factors are involved in determining how often you should have your skates sharpened: how often you skate, how heavy you are, the hollow you require, and the quality of your blades.

Choosing the Blade

There are many different types of blades on the market, and the type of skating that you will be doing will decide which blade is for you.

Figure skating requires maximum maneuverability and a blade that has a shorter radius than a hockey or speed skate. The toepicks also vary from unobtrusive to deeply defined. The width of the figure-skating blade is thicker than that of a hockey or speed skate, too. The length of the blade runs from the tip of the toe to the very edge of the heel. It should cover the full length of the sole of the boot. To ensure the greatest degree of stability for the skater, it is better to choose a pair of skates with a blade slightly too long, rather than too short.

Rigorous skating requires a precision ground blade with a hollow that is free from flats and edges that are not uniform. The more precise the edge, the more controlled the skating. Sharpening or side-honing (a term rarely used) will ensure a better edge and reduce the weight of the blade, but this is mainly for very advanced skating.

Specialist Blades

Compulsory Figures. Figure blades are needed to perform exact compulsory figures. A figure blade must be shallow ground in order to prevent double tracings. Toepicks should also be a little higher to avoid catching on loops and marring clean tracings.

Free Skating. Free skating requires many athletic maneuvers such as jumps, spins, and combination movements. This type of skating requires larger toepicks and one large toepick to give a good bite for jumping. The hollow of a free-skating blade is ground extra deep to prevent slipping, and the blade is sharpened for maximum edge. The skate is strong and rugged, yet light in weight (accomplished by removing all unnecessary steel).

Ice Dancing. Accomplished ice dancers require a blade that gives them peak performance. The blade heel is shorter to avoid skate collision during intricate dance steps and overlap footwork. And the blades are sharpened to a thin width for high-speed movements with a minimum of effort.

Setting the Blade

Setting the blade is the term used to define the placing of the blade in the correct position on the sole of the boot. Most matched sets of skates that come from the factory have the blades already mounted, but you can look for separate boots and blades. Better boots and blades come separately because equipment manufacturers usually specialize in either one or the other product.

When shopping for a pair of skates, look for blades that are screwed on and not riveted on. If you need an adjustment and repositioning of the blade, it will be necessary to unscrew the blade, fill the holes, and remount it on the sole of the boot.

Cheaper boots would be all right if both the blades were positioned correctly, but often it is necessary to remount one of the blades.

At times, many beginners seem to be skating on their ankles. A simple repositioning of the blade could solve many of their problems. The blade shouldn't be set down the center of the sole of the boot, but rather to the inside of the midline. This helps to offset the tendency skat-

ers have to drop their ankles in.

Occasionally, the reverse is true—a beginner's ankles will go to the outside. Then it is necessary to move the blade to the outside of the boot or put in a "heel lift" on the outside of each heel. If your skates are returned to you after setting without all the screws in place, it is so that you can test the setting in case it still needs some altering. When you are totally satisfied with the setting, you can have all the screws set in.

LACING

The lacing of the boot is as important as the quality of the boot itself. Improper lacing will make even a good boot feel as though it doesn't fit.

Do not lace the boot too tightly around the toes or at the top. The tightest part of the lacing should be around the ankle.

When a boot is properly laced, you should be able to insert two fingers under the tongue at the top. But the laces at the ankle area should fit snugly and hold the boot securely to the foot. Don't let the boot swim around on your foot: it should be snug and your heel should not slip up and down.

CARE OF EQUIPMENT

Skates need a certain amount of care to promote long life. Besides having the blades sharpened by a professional regularly, there are also a few other points to remember.

Always wear skate guards when you are not on the ice. This will prevent nicking of the sharpened blade surface. The rubber models are fine.

The guards should be removed when storing the skates. This will prevent rusting of the blade. A change in temperature from the ice rink to the indoors can cause condensation to accumulate on the blade.

The boot and especially the blade should be cleaned and wiped dry after each use. Use a good quality cleaner on the boot that is water **repellent and will restore the condition of the leather.**

Good clothing choices reflect the mood and subject matter of the performance.

The heel and sole should be covered every so often with an application of a special type of enamel (purchased at any professional skating shop) to prevent the separation of the heel and the outer sole layers and to keep the sole and heel from rotting should water seep in.

Always check to see that the screws on the bottom are secure and haven't loosened. Loose screws will allow water to seep in, causing rust that will eventually cause a screw to lose its thread, not to mention the danger of the blade dropping off while skating.

CLOTHING

Today, any styles and any colors are acceptable on the ice for "pleasure skating." Outdoor skating will, of course, require warmer clothing than that used for an indoor rink. Men usually wear stretch pants (not too tight fitting) and a sweater, but women prefer a leotard with short skating skirt.

Carry a heavier sweater for rest periods. Beginners require gloves, which are as important for warmth, as they are for protection.

If wearing a hat for outdoor skating, choose one that fits close to the head. Women should avoid securing their hair with bobby pins that might fall out onto the ice, causing skaters to fall.

Freestyle skaters performing in front of an audience will want their costumes to be pleasing to the eye. Judges should not mark for what a skater wears, but they are subconsciously influenced by overall appearance.

Women tend to favor chiffon, Lycra, and other soft stretch fabrics with sequins adding sparkle and flash to an outfit. Men have become more inventive with their outfits lately, with one-piece jump suits in various colors favored over the staid all-black outfits previously worn.

Remember that fine detail work on an outfit will not be seen from a distance. A good cut to an outfit will do far more than fancy or frilly ornamentation. Especially if one tends to be on the heavy side, stay away from light colors, shiny fabrics, or patterns.

And if the appearance is going to be televised, take note that white, black, or dazzling outfits will be hard to see when viewed on the television screen. While most people have color television sets nowadays, black and white televisions transmit colors such as red and blue at the same intensity. So your outfit that is colorful and contrasting in person will look drab with indistinguishable colors on black and white TV.

Boots should be clean; they can ruin the entire appearance of a stunning outfit if they are dirty and scuffed. And always check to make sure that the laces are tied properly and tucked inside the boot before starting out. A loose or broken lace can cause an unnecessary spill and ruin your performance.

Outfits should blend into your routine and not stand out so much that they become obvious and upstage your performance. After all, it is your skating abilities with which you want the audience or judges to be impressed.

3

Professionalism: Pro or Not

Whether you become involved in competition or merely plan a routine for your own enjoyment, remain aware of the presentation. Someone is always watching you—even when you aren't aware of it.

If you are skating for yourself only, your ultimate goal will be to glide effortlessly around the ice. To attain that end and to feel as though what you are doing comes naturally will take hours and hours of practice. Start from the beginning by developing a pleasant look on your face. While intricate maneuvers demand intense concentration, you should never appear to be concentrating so much that it looks as though what you are doing has stopped being fun.

And, if you start from the very beginning by wearing a smile, you'll feel more confident and relaxed than if you are straining with every move. Practice looking happy, confident, and relaxed. That way, if you ever do enter any form of competition, it will be that much easier to relax on the ice, even when you are overcome

with butterflies in the stomach the first few times out.

Judges score high for effortless, smooth routines that have that "finished" quality. The skater who looks too studious on the ice or the skater who appears to be anxious with every move will score low. You must appear to be in total control of the ice.

Whether in competition, skating a show, or just skating a routine for your own enjoyment, you should always strive for a professional attitude.

Always be aware of the other skater and learn to share and be courteous with the ice you are using. Too often we see a skater swear, kick a hole in the ice with the heel of his blade, or display some other form of immature behavior when another skater has gotten in the way.

Be on time for your lessons and/or rehearsal.

Nearly all performers, at one time or another, have the tendency to get down on themselves. Everyone makes errors. We must learn to accept this fact. As a professional, Fran Dorsey says,

"I often am very hard on myself, much more so than on anyone else; and it's very difficult for me to accept and deal with any mistake I make. My feeling is that it's okay for others to make errors, but it's inexcusable for me to do so. Naturally, any mistake—especially stumbling or falling on the ice—is most damaging to one's ego. The skater must learn to accept these mistakes, however embarrassing, with a mature attitude, and certainly must not be so childish or unprofessional as to pout, stomp or kick the ice, or not finish the program. This is most unprofessional, whether it occurs in a competition or in an amateur ice show. It is absolutely unforgivable in a professional show." People don't like to be around any person with that type of attitude. It takes only one incident of that type on the ice to mark a skater as unpleasant and temperamental for the rest of his career.

If you should fall, don't let it ruin the rest of your performance. Always recover with a quick smile and pick up the beat of the music, then forget about the mistake and continue with the rest of your routine. There isn't a skater who has set a blade on the ice who hasn't taken a fall in front of an audience. The very best take a spill from time to time. Just pick yourself up as quickly as possible and continue with your performance. Self-control and restraint are the magic words if a skater is to maintain a professional attitude. The goal is to make all your skating maneuvers seem effortless, yet full of emotion and style. This isn't an athletic event, but an artistic performance.

TIPS ON FREESTYLE PERFORMING

Freestyle skating is one of the most popular forms of ice-skating. Freestyle skating, or free skating, means that the movements the skater performs and the sequence in which he or she performs them are not limited or restricted.

When in competition, you should incorporate as many difficult moves into your routine as possible within the time allotted to gain the highest possible score. The marks are awarded for technical merit—the difficulty of achievement and sequence—and for artistic impression.

For noncompetitive exhibitions, doing what looks spectacular within your range of ability is the main objective. Be aware, though, that it takes hard work to succeed in looking free and graceful and months of practice to lose that look of being tense, nervous, and too aware of what you are doing.

Types of Freestyle Skating

Freestyle skating consists of three types of performances: solo, pair, and ice dancing. Each, discussed at length in later chapters, consists of various types of movements.

Freestyle skating consists of various types of spirals, spins, jumps, and spread eagles. Each successive generation of skaters is jumping higher and better than the previous one, as technique is perfected for intricate advanced moves. But, jumping and spinning are not mastered overnight; it takes long, hard hours, and many spills to develop your skills.

Linking steps or footwork are used to run your spirals, jumps, and spins together. It doesn't matter how limited your abilities are. If you can perform the simplest jump, spin, and spiral, you can work out a routine that you can improve as you learn more advanced technical movements.

Freestyle Creativity

The individuality of a skater's performance can only be expressed through the personal creativity of the skater. From the beginning, try to plan your routines by yourself: don't rely always on someone more experienced to plan out your moves.

Watch what others are doing and use parts of their routines with added touches of your own. Study the way in which you execute your spins and jumps, and then work out innovative ways to get yourself into position.

Avoid being stereotyped as "There's Mary Smith's pupil." Don't become an expressionless skating robot. After all, free skating should be a means of self-expression. No two skaters approach a jump the same way, therefore it is impossible to copy someone exactly. Try to develop your own technique.

By all means, freestyle skating should be fun. The more you practice, the more relaxed you will be with yourself and your movements. This in turn will enable you to have a better time skating.

Don't fall into the trap of only skating those moves that you know well and not trying anything different. Always incorporate one or two new maneuvers into your routine that you can work at along with the rest of your "better" moves. This way you will always be advancing and improving your abilities.

4

Preparing a Program

As your basic skating technique improves, and jumps, spins, and footwork seem to flow together on the ice, you'll want to start preparing some type of routine in which you can weave it all together. Select a piece of music that you feel comfortable with and that has a mood and tempo that fit the maneuvers you have mastered.

If your repertoire is limited, it is better to skate a short program to music that has a medium to slow tempo. Music that is too fast can force you to trip all over your feet.

Don't stretch your routine just to have time on the ice. Keep it short, as it is always best to leave an audience wanting to see more. Plan movements that are concise and interesting to hold the attention of the audience. As you improve, your choice of routines can vary in tempo and difficulty. Arrange the jumps and spins so that they are evenly spaced out. Give yourself time to breathe between difficult moves.

CREATING A SKATING PATTERN

No matter what form of skating you will be doing—freestyle, figure, pair, or ice dancing—it will be necessary to create a pattern in which to skate. The more inventive a skater is, the more exciting his or her program will be. Look for unusual ways to link movements; don't always stick to the same old way of doing things.

Many times, in their eagerness to show off their technical ability, skaters fail to discover the best way to present their jumps and spins. Not only is sequence important, but also the portion of the rink in which a move is performed: each move should be viewed to its best advantage.

A strong start and an impressive finish are important. The first thing you should do when planning a program is arrange the opening and closing of the routine. Choose movements for the closing that you can do when slightly tired. Begin with easy maneuvers so you can get the feel of the ice and warm up a little. Try to put the most difficult maneuvers in the first half of the program, during which you will still have most of your strength. Blend the rest of the program with intervals of jumps and spins, linked with attractive steps, spirals, and a spread eagle or a bauer. Space the highlights in the program to match your personal moments of strength and fatigue. These will vary according to each skater's physique and stamina.

An important thing to remember, whether skating at the neighborhood ice rink or in competition, is that you should know the rink you are skating on and use it to its best advantage. Plan to use all of the ice area and avoid the tendency to cram too much activity into one part of the rink.

To plan out your program, first compile a list of all the technical movements that you can do. Then rewrite the list and number the movements in what seems to be a good order to perform them, according to your own physical strength. On a piece of paper, draw a rectangle with the dimensions of the ice rink you will be performing in, and mark the number of a movement at the position you think is best to perform it. In this manner, you can see if your program is spaced out equally over the whole ice surface.

STRIVING FOR QUALITY, NOT QUANTITY

Throughout your program, quality must be consistent. It won't be if too many of your best moves are packed into the beginning. A good performance can be ruined by a mediocre finish: always let the program build to an exciting conclusion.

A program consisting of neatly planned and well performed moves will look better than one that contains difficult steps performed poorly. In competition, marks are awarded for artistic creativity, as well as for technical merit.

An advanced skater should be careful not to overcrowd his routine with too many jumps and spins. Assemble your program so that it will have continuity. An audience can become easily bored by too much of a good thing: create a setting for each maneuver.

GEOGRAPHICAL PLANNING

When planning your routine, it is necessary to present your difficult moves at highlight points in the rink. Spins and jumps look better in the center of the rink or at either end (assuming you are working in a rectangular area).

The fast-paced, split jump should be done in the middle of the rink so that the audience gets to see a good profile of the skater. And a spin is better appreciated if executed not too far from the spectators, yet not too close to the railing.

Try to fill the entire rink surface with moves. If too many of your moves are done at one end of the rink, the audience at the opposite corner will feel overlooked. Avoid skating too close to the wall because the spectators sitting up front will not be able to see your moves. Spirals and linking steps or footwork should be used so that your routine doesn't give the impression of moving too much in the same direction.

In keeping time to your music, you can vary the tempo by altering your speed. Holding your audience's attention is easier if you switch back and forth from a fast to a slow tempo.

You will be concentrating on your difficult maneuvers; practice them over and over so that they become familiar in the way in which you have worked them into your routine. The more familiar you are with your various jumps, spins, and footwork, the more you will exude self-confidence on the ice. The less you have to concentrate on the technical aspects of your skating, the more you can concentrate on achieving an artistic performance.

5
Choosing the Music

Music is an integral part of every free-skating, pair-skating, and ice-dancing routine. You must have the right piece of music in which to place your moves, because even a good ear can't place moves in music that doesn't fit them. And even the finest of jumps will be lost if it is a split-second off the time of the music. That is why it is so important to choose a piece of music that fits exactly the speed at which you are able to skate. Ending your performance exactly with the last beat of the music is critical, too.

If the music that you have picked does not, even in a small way, inspire your skating, then you have undoubtedly picked the wrong piece of music. It should also be pleasing to the audience.

Choosing something that is easily identifiable and well liked makes it easy for the audience to follow. But no matter what you choose, always pick music that you can skate to without too much difficulty.

Find music that expresses a mood—happiness, sadness, strength, humor—and your task of making a routine expressive will be easier. The greatest compliment a skater can receive is, "Your skating was so fascinating that I forgot you were on skates."

Not only the feet are important to expressiveness on ice, but also the hands, face, arms, shoulders, and legs. While a relaxed smile permanently fixed on the face is more desirable than anxiety displayed through clenched teeth, the emotion of the routine and of the music should be mirrored on the face. A knowledge of ballet is helpful with arm and body movement. Most successful skaters have studied ballet for years to achieve fluid arm movements.

Expand your appreciation of music. Start listening to radio stations with classical, blues, and jazz pieces. Attend concerts to hear pieces live and plan your skating maneuvers in your mind while listening. Try skating to various types of music to see which best suits your skating style.

There should be a close relationship between the feeling, style, and tempo of the music and what the skater is physically doing on the ice. Remember, you are interpreting the music. If the music is slow, with long flowing lines, and you are wildly jumping and spinning, or if the music is very rhythmic and dynamic and you are skating smoothly, perhaps you should look for a piece of music that better says what you are trying to express. Music is only the medium for presentation of your skating abilities.

The ability to interpret music is learned; the skater must become sensitive to what music is saying. Listen and feel for the places in the music where it says "jump," where it calls for a spin, or where it nudges you to skate in a long, flowing, balletic style. The words of the song should help you to tell your story. When the piece of music and the skater say the same things, you have an artistic performance. When they don't—the music goes one way and the skater another—the result is a confused audience.

Women should try to choose music that is sung by a female singer or performed on an instrument that sounds feminine. The opposite applies to men.

The emotion of the routine and the music should be mirrored in the entire body. Your body should express all the feelings of the music, and you should use your face as an actor or actress would, baring his emotions for the world to see. Your arms and hands also play a major part in expressing the mood of the words and music.

Skate to different types of music so that you aren't perceived as being able to perform only one style of skating. Branching into other areas of skating, such as jazz and rock, will alleviate boredom. To be cast always as a ballerina, when you've had a secret desire to do jazz, can be limiting.

When planning your costume, coordinate it with the style of music to which you are skating. The costume helps to set the mood, whether it's classical, jazz, or roaring twenties. And before performing in front of an audience, practice in your costume at least once to make certain that it is easy to work in. You don't want to wait until that important moment to find out you have problems with the outfit. Too many embarrassing moments could have been avoided if a skater had taken the time to try out the costume before the performance.

It is essential to be able to skate to your music in a relaxed manner. If the hours of preparation can be sensed by the audience, then you have not prepared enough. Your routine should glide across the ice, and you should appear as though you had simply dropped from the heavens, onto the ice. It should all be effortless and, moreover, you should be happy.

6
Skating Fundamentals

TERMS

Before starting with any of the maneuvers, some basic terminology must be explained so that you will understand what it is you are being asked to do.

Each skating maneuver consists of various positions. The *first position* helps to control your edge and comes immediately after the initial push. The *second position* of an edge comes by rotating or changing your arms and shoulders so that the free arm and free leg will pass to the front or back depending on whether the skater is going forward or backward. The free leg and free arm always pass through at the same time.

The *free arm* and *free leg* are the parts of the skater's body that are not engaged in skating. They are opposite the *skating arm* and *skating leg*.

The *prepared position* is the correct position of the body just before a turn, jump, spin, or change of edge.

The *checked position* counteracts the natural rotation, or swing, set up by a turn, edge, jump, or spin. A check is made by rotating your arms, hips, and shoulders against the pull of a turn so that you can hold position without being pulled off your line of travel.

STROKING

Proper stroking is a basic skill essential for a polished look. It is also very important to acquire this skill prior to attempting the routines at the end of this book. If you can confidently perform the following exercise, you are ready to continue with more advanced skating movements.

For proper forward stroking, begin with your weight centered over your blades, and skate forward in a "zigzag" pattern. At the beginning of each stroke your feet should be close together, your head, shoulders, and back should be erect, from the waist up, and your arms should be extended at your sides, just a little bit in front of your body. Your knees should be slightly bent, and your weight should be resting on the very center of the skating blades.

With your knees flexed to absorb the shock, turn the right foot out so that the entire blade is in contact with the ice. Next, push with the side of the right blade (the right inside edge) without allowing the blade of the pushing foot to slip on the ice.

It's important to remember that you shouldn't push with the toepick. Glide forward on the left skating foot, keeping your skating knee bent and your weight on the middle of the blade of the skating foot. Your arms should be at chest level, extended to the sides, and you should be skating at a slight angle or from corner to corner.

As you glide on the left foot, the right leg becomes fully extended with toe pointed down, turned out to the side, and free of all its weight; you slowly return the right free leg and foot to the beginning position, rising up and straightening the left skating leg so that the right free leg will be able to return to its position without catching the toepick on the ice. During the return, the blade of the right skate is kept parallel to the ice surface, and the foot turns evenly in and is brought close and parallel to the skating foot.

If the center of gravity is over the middle of the left skating foot at all times, even when the right foot is behind there will be no chance of falling. To ensure this, always keep your skating knee bent. Your head should be up and looking forward, and your arms should be used for balance, extended on either side of the body at shoulder height, over the left skating blade. As a basic rule in skating, remember that the skating leg is always bent, and the free leg is usually straight with toe pointed out to the side.

Next comes the element of obtaining maximum power from the pushing while keeping a smooth and effortless action. A powerful push, or takeoff, can be obtained only by keeping the weight of the body over the pushing skate. Pushing from a standing position is easy because you have plenty of time to position yourself correctly. The difficulty comes when you are already in motion.

A moving push requires time and distance to execute; weight must be transferred smoothly from the pushing foot to the new skating foot. This pushing with the free foot and gliding on the skating foot is called *forward stroking*.

BASIC EDGES

In order to make turns on the ice, you must be able to use the edge of the skating blade correctly. To do this you must understand how a blade is constructed. The blade of a skate has three main parts: the outside edge, the inside edge, and the middle (or flat). To skate a curve you must be on an edge. You attain an edge by shifting and dropping your ankle slightly in the direction that you want the blade to go and by shifting or "leaning" your body in the direction of the curve you are skating.

Forward Outside Edge

To attain a left forward outside edge, your left ankle drops down slightly to the outside of the skate. Your left arm is forward. The right arm is in back and parallel to the ice, and the right free leg is behind.

Your left hand should be held over the curve you are about to make, and your shoulders should make an angle of about forty-five degrees with this same line. The right arm and shoulder will follow the line of your shoulders and remain outside the curve. With your weight over the middle of the left skating foot, your right foot should be free to extend behind you. It should leave the ice about a skate's length behind you, with the instep turned directly over the tracing line. Your hands should be carried at chest level, with the palms facing down toward the ice and the fingers relaxed. Your head should be looking in the direction that you are traveling. This is called the basic forward outside edge position, or the first position.

When you finally are able to get onto the edge, you will notice the difficulty of holding your position. Your body will tend to rotate to the inside of the curve. The free leg will tend to pass to the outside of the curve rather than staying on it or over the tracing you are making, and your free arm will want to come forward. This is known as *swing*, or *over-rotation*, and is

THE LEFT FORWARD OUTSIDE EDGE . . . in first position **(left)**, the left arm is in front and the right free arm and leg extended in back over the tracing. For the second position **(right)**, shoulders have rotated. The right free arm and leg have been brought through to the front and extended over the tracing. The left arm has moved back.

a skater's worst enemy. It takes continued practice to maintain edges. Your first half-circles will undoubtedly be shallow. As you become more controlled, you should try to reduce them to about three times your own height.

The easiest way to see if you are following your line of travel is to look down at your skating hand to see if it is still in your basic starting position, aiming in the direction you are traveling. The free hand and arm should be extended behind, over the free leg. You should have no arm or shoulder movement at all. This is the first position on the outside edge.

If you notice that your blade tends to skid, then your weight is too far forward on the blade, or you have transferred from the outside edge to the middle, or flat, or even the inside edge of the blade. Try to keep your weight back at all times.

When you have an outside edge in first position under control, move on to the second position. To reach the second position, you rotate your shoulders and bring your right arm and shoulder forward. At the very same time, you swing the right free leg through to the front, over the curve you are starting on; the left arm and shoulder rotate to the back.

Maintaining control of all edges and turns is called *checking*. Each position must be held steady and checked before moving on to the next position.

As you swing the right leg through to the front, be sure to pass it closely past your left skating leg, nearly touching your skating ankle, or your body will over-rotate in the direction of the curve. Also, you must be careful not to swing your hips through to the front. Any of these errors will pull you off your edge.

When practicing edges try to obtain the edge immediately, rather than going from the flat to the edge of the blade. An edge is made by leaning. When practicing edges, don't steer the edge as if you were going around a corner in a car—lean into the turn.

If you lose your balance at any point, bend your skating knee down and over the outside edge, rather than straightening up, which will be your first instinct. Keeping your center of gravity low and your knees bent to absorb the shocks will keep you from falling.

Forward Inside Edge

To skate a right forward inside edge, first practice making a two-footed curve to the left. Your left arm will be forward and inside the curve. In other words, you have your left arm forward while skating on your right foot. The free foot and arm are always opposite to the inside edge the skater is on. The right arm will follow the line of the shoulders and be outside the curve (your shoulders are still being held square to the line of travel).

As soon as you have this position, let your left foot come off the ice and position it behind the skating foot and inside the curve you are skating. If the back end of the skating blade of the free foot is slightly inside the tracing, your free foot is in the correct position. Your hips should be square to the line of travel: don't let the free hip swing behind you. To fight against a swing of the body, you should think of the free

hip as being placed a little forward. This is the first position of the forward inside edge.

The second position is made by rotating the right arm and shoulder through to the front along with the left free leg. At the same time, the left free arm passes through to the back. Again, remember that the left free leg must pass very closely by the right skating leg.

Practice this position for both the left and right legs—left forward inside edge and right forward inside edge.

Forward Crossovers

Forward crossovers in later stages will be used to pick up speed on a curve. A crossover is exactly what the name implies—a crossing of the free foot around in front of the skating foot. Crossovers should be practiced clockwise and counterclockwise with equal strength.

For a right forward outside crossover you will be skating counterclockwise, skate onto a left outside edge, with your right free arm and shoulder forward and your left skating arm back. Hold this position; then pass your right free foot in a circular movement around and in front of the toe of your skating foot. Do not pick the free foot up high and place it over your skating foot. When you can, place it inside and parallel to the curve on a right forward inside edge.

As your weight goes onto the right foot, bend your right knee and push with the outside edge of your left blade. This push is made toward the outside of the curve and almost parallel to the right foot. Ideally, the left foot remains straight throughout the entire push of the outside edge, and it even progresses slightly forward during the push. A strong, left outside push can only be executed if the right knee is deeply bent. First, the left foot is lifted off the ice by a slight straightening of the right leg (with the heel held down and the toe up to prevent catching the toepicks). Then, while the left foot is lifted off the ice, the left leg remains straight until it is brought into position alongside the right skating foot. Both knees should start to bend again, and a normal stroke is made while you prepare to repeat the action.

Errors are made by pushing off with the toepick of the left foot instead of with the entire left outside edge, and by straightening the right knee as a crossover is made.

While the movement is called a cross*over,* if you step *over* your skating foot instead of *around* it, your balance will be thrown off and your hips will not be square to the line that you are traveling. For a smooth crossover, the free blade should be kept low and parallel to the ice surface. Don't bring it up over the skating foot.

Now try a clockwise left forward outside crossover. This time start on your right forward outside edge, with your left arm and shoulder forward. Bring your left foot around in front of your right, onto a left forward inside edge. At the same time, push from the outside edge of the right skating blade. Bring your feet together again and stroke onto the right forward outside blade while you prepare to repeat the crossover action. This stroke is important because it positions the body and squares it to the line you are traveling. Always remember to bend the left knee as it comes around to take the weight so that the right foot can make a strong push onto an outside edge. During the right push, the right free leg and knee straighten and progress slightly forward. They are brought back into position by a straightening of the left leg.

Back Crossovers

You do back crossovers much as you do forward crossovers, except that you skate backward and slide one foot across in front of the other foot. Start by moving backward on both feet in a counterclockwise direction. Your right arm should be strongly checked behind your body, and your head looking toward the center of the circle. Transfer your weight to the right skating foot. Make a semicircular push with your left foot (as you will do for the back edges), but this time instead of lifting the foot off the ice, continue to slide or bring it around in front of the right foot. As you transfer your weight onto the left foot, you lift the right foot off the ice behind you (without making a toe scratch) and place it inside the curve, parallel to but well inside and behind the left heel. This movement is then repeated to continue skating backward.

Remember not to pick the left foot up *over* the right foot; this results in a clumsy appearance. The left foot should at all times be brought smoothly *around* in front of the skating-foot, never leaving the ice.

You will eventually learn to get a stronger push from the outside edge of the foot that has crossed behind. This can only be practiced after you have mastered the back crossover and are confident with it. This weight transference is subtle; if you practice it before you are ready, you will end up scratching the toepicks on the ice. Try to correct this by pushing down with the back of the heel until you eliminate all toe scratching.

Back crossovers should be practiced in a clockwise direction, starting with your right foot crossing in front of your left. To start, move backward on both feet in a clockwise direction, with your right arm in front and your left shoulder and arm pulled back in a checked position along the line of travel. Your head is looking to the center of the circle. Push with the back inside edge of your right foot and, without lifting it off the ice, slide it across in front of the left foot. The left foot—now on the back outside edge—is lifted gently off the ice and placed onto the ice well inside the curve, behind the right skating heel. The left foot is now on the back outside edge again. Repeat this move to continue traveling in a clockwise direction.

Before you can proceed with any of the following steps, it is important that you have mastered the basic edges and crossovers. Confidence in these moves will allow you to concentrate on the intricate steps that follow. Don't rush yourself: build a firm base in the beginning or you will be unsuccessful with the jumps, spins, and connecting moves that come later.

Backward Outside Edges

It goes without saying that you have to have a basic understanding and feel of skating backward before you can progress to intricate backward edges.

For a left backward outside edge, push off onto your left outside edge. Your arms and shoulders should be turned in slightly to the left. Your legs should be just a skate's length apart.

THE LEFT BACK OUTSIDE EDGE . . . in first position **(left)**, the right arm and left free leg are extended in front over the tracing. The left arm is behind. Notice how the body faces toward the inside of the circle you are skating. In the second position **(right)**, the right arm, right free leg, and head move to the back over the tracing and the left arm moves to the front at a slight angle across the chest. The body position has changed from facing the inside of the semicircle to facing the outside of the circle.

For a pushoff, the back inside edge of the right pushing foot makes a semicircular cut, or take-off, as you strike onto a left back outside edge. The shoulders are rotated strongly to the left (or toward the inside of the semicircle you are skating). Your left arm and right free leg are extended over the tracing in front, with your left arm in back. This is your first position of the left backward outside edge.

This push is difficult because the semicircular push on takeoff made by the right foot is in a clockwise direction, which tends to pull the body around in that direction. As the right foot makes this takeoff you must turn against the pull by putting your hips and upper body toward the inside of the circle in a counterclock-

wise direction. With the right free foot and leg in a forward position over the tracing instead of behind the skating foot, it will be difficult to face the inside of the circle.

The second position is made by skating the last half of the semicircle, bringing your right arm and free leg slowly and smoothly to the back, and, at the same time, turning your head to follow in the same direction in conjunction with the right arm and free leg. The left arm moves toward the front of the body and over the tracing. Your body position is actually changing from facing into the semicircle in the first position, to facing outside the semicircle in the second position.

The backward takeoff can be practiced by

pushing and lifting the right free leg and foot up in a pigeon-toed fashion.

Practice the right back outside edge by reversing the instruction for the right foot. Remember, too, that to get full power from a push the weight must stay over the pushing foot until the last possible moment.

Backward Inside Edges

To execute backward inside edges, start on the flat of your blades with your feet a skate's length apart and your arms slightly to the left. To push off, transfer your weight to the right foot and lift your left foot and bring it next to the right for the takeoff. Now make the semi-circular push with the right foot, and step down onto the right back inside edge, turning your arms to the left (your right shoulder should be forward). Lift the right free leg and extend it over the tracing in front of your body. This is

In the second position the right free foot is drawn in toward the left skating foot. Your hips will start rotating against your shoulders, but your body remains in the same direction.

LEFT BACK INSIDE EDGE . . . in the first position push off with your right foot and transfer your weight onto your left skating foot. You push off into a left back inside edge turning your arms and shoulders slightly to the left leaning against the edge. The right free leg is extended up and in front over the tracing. You are beginning to skate a square in the first position.

LEFT BACKWARD INSIDE EDGE

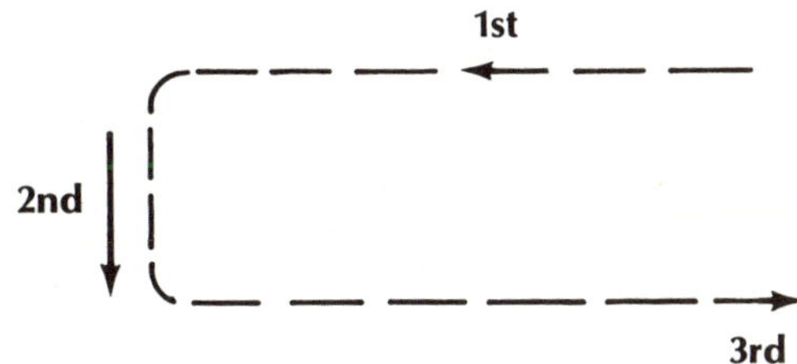

part of the first position and is also part of a square you will be executing as you skate across the ice.

The back inside edge, if not controlled when you lean into the circle to strike back onto the

In the third position you skate back across the ice to complete the square you have skated. Both arms and shoulders are extended to the right over the right free leg which is now extended in back over the tracing.

inside edge, will pull you out and off the edge. To do this move successfully, your hips should rotate against your shoulders, with your body facing the same way all the time.

Next, to execute the second position correctly you must lean into the circle so that you ride onto the back inside edge of the blade. The right foot is drawn in toward the skating foot, almost brushing it, as you draw the second pattern of square, skating down the ice (still backward).

This edge has a third position. It occurs when you come back across the ice in the direction from which you started, *i.e.,* completing a square. Both arms and shoulders are extended to the right over the right free leg. Your body will be facing in the same direction throughout all three position changes.

Reverse the procedure for executing the right back inside edge.

7

Freestyle Skating

Freestyle skating, also called free skating, is fast becoming one of the most popular types of skating. The jumps and spins explained in this chapter must be practiced until each one can be performed strongly and with total control. Any weak moves will hinder your performance of the next position.

Assuming that you have the skating fundamentals mastered, you are now ready to progress to more advanced movements on the ice. Before going on to these intermediate movements, you should be able to stop and start on the ice, get up off the ice when you fall, be able to do forward stroking (push with one foot and glide on the other), and skate backward. Balance is an all-important factor when doing jumps and spins. Do not attempt to do anything on the ice until you are able to skate steadily forward and backward around the rink, without feeling wobbly or uncertain of yourself.

While this book can be used as a self-teaching aid, it is always a good idea to take professional skating lessons in conjunction with your personal efforts. When trying to learn the more advanced movements, it will be impossible to turn pages and skate at the same time. More than that, though, mastering advanced techniques requires an educated eye to tell you what you are doing wrong so that you do not formulate bad habits that might be carried into your advanced skating routines. The earlier bad habits are caught, the easier they are to do away with.

FREESTYLE TECHNIQUES

The basic freestyle technique incorporates jumps, spins, spirals, and connecting moves into one uniform and flowing program. These steps are linked in a sequence and accompanied by music to express a mood.

The effortless grace that freestyle skaters display takes years to develop. There is no way to shortcut the hours and hours of practice that go into developing a personal style.

If your routines seem jerky and choppy, then you know that you need more practice before going on to something new. If you are not able to execute the first part of a move with ease and confidence, then, certainly, don't go on to the second part.

As in any sport, excellence cannot be rushed. You have to develop muscles that haven't been used before. Acquiring a new balance and center of gravity while moving will take time and work. So let's get started.

TURNS

3-Turns

A 3-turn derives its name from the tracing it makes on fresh ice—in the shape of a 3. It can be done both forward to backward and backward to forward, from an outside to an inside edge or an inside to an outside edge. This is a balletic turn and is graceful when performed correctly.

Forward Outside 3-Turn. Fortunately, the direction of rotation is the same as the natural swing of the edge. If you are traveling on an outside edge on a curve, your skating foot keeps following this same direction. Because it is done on a curve, a turn started on a forward outside edge reverses and ends up on the same curve going backward on a backward inside edge. There are three basic positions in a 3-turn.

3-TURN

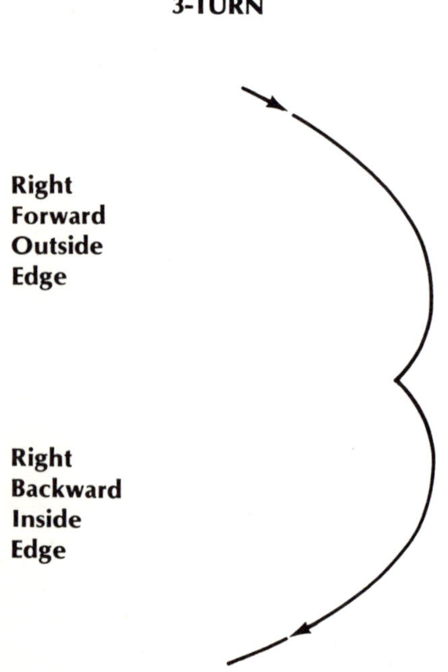

To do a right forward outside 3-turn, push onto a right forward outside edge, in first position. Next, you move into the second position by bringing your left free arm and shoulder strongly forward, and pressing your right skating arm and shoulder backward. Bring your left free foot in, to touch the heel of your skating foot, without altering your line of travel. You should be looking toward the center of the circle, as you do when making all circles and curves.

The change of direction comes when you have turned your hip against your shoulder (like twisting a glove between your hands). The pressure of your hips twisting against your shoulders will cause you to turn swiftly and sharply in the other direction. Remember that you are on an outside edge and you will rise up slightly on the right knee to make the turn, shifting forward for the turn to the area between the ball and bottom toepick of the skating foot, then returning to a slightly bent-knee position when exiting on the right, back inside edge. It is a sit-lift-sit motion. You sit for the forward outside edge, lift for the turn, and sit again for the backward inside edge.

If you are having a hard time turning, then you simply haven't exerted enough pressure with your shoulders against your hips, or transferred your weight correctly during the turn. The more pressure, the easier it will be to turn. You must allow a certain time for the pressure to build up before you try to turn: don't rush the turn.

As you make this turn, your left free foot remains touching your skating heel. However, immediately upon completing the turn and exiting on a right back inside edge, extend the left free leg out to the back in check position. You should now be pressing your left free arm, shoulder, and hip back. Your head is still looking toward the center of the circle. The left side will be in a strong open, or checked position, with the right arm perpendicular to the body. This is your third position.

Try to achieve a more defined 3 when making the turn. Avoid making your 3-turns in tiny circles, or you'll never learn to cover the ice at a good speed.

If, after you have made the turn from the checked position, you rise up onto the toepick,

RIGHT FORWARD OUTSIDE 3-TURN . . . after skating the first position, or forward right outside edge, in the second position (**left**), you rotate the shoulders and turn your body until it faces the inside of the circle, the left arm is in front over the tracing. The left free leg is tucked in to the heel of the right skating leg. The right arm is in back. You are preparing to use the pressure of the shoulders against the hips. In the third position (**right**), having executed the turn, you are on a right back inside edge in a checked position. Your left free arm, shoulder, and hip are in back with the left leg extending over the tracing. Your right arm, shoulder, hip, and head are turned toward the center of the circle you have just skated. To maintain this position, and other checked positions after turns, takes many hours of practice.

it is because you are leaning forward. You don't yet know how to skate backward well enough. Or you might have shifted your weight too far forward onto the toepicks.

Another common error occurs when the skater allows the free leg to swing forward before the turn. This causes a loss of balance and a nasty fall backward. Repeat the above in reverse for left forward outside 3-turn.

Forward Inside 3-Turn. Start out on your right forward inside edge in your first position (left free arm forward, right arm back, and your left free leg extended slightly inside the tracing). For the second position, turn into the circle, rotate the hips against the shoulders, and bring

the toe of the left free foot into the heel of the right skating foot. Shift your weight forward for the turn. Upon completion of the turn, exit on a right outside back edge, with arms and shoulders and head facing inside the circle for the third position. The left free leg extends in back over the tracing. Repeat the above in reverse for the left foot.

Backward Outside 3-Turn. Facing the inside of the circle, start out on your left backward outside edge in first position. For the second position, turn to the outside of the circle, rotating the head, shoulders, and upper body against the hips. The skating knee should be bent, and the free leg in front and over the tracing for this second position. As you apply the pressure to the hips and momentarily check the hips against the shoulders to make the turn, lift yourself up, *i.e.,* lift yourself up and finish on the same foot but it has now become a forward inside edge, with shoulders, arms, and head facing outside the circle. It is important that the free leg remains in front for the entire turn, and is extended well over the tracing to the outside of the exit edge for the third position.

Unless you are capable of a strong backward edge, do not attempt this turn without the aid of a teacher. If you don't keep your weight toward the middle of the blade, as you skate the back outside edge of the circle, you will fall backward. When entering the turn, press your skating knee down, and then lift up for the turn. Transfer your weight toward the heel of the blade for the turn, then sink down, again, onto the middle of the blade for the new forward inside edge.

Again, it should be a sit-lift-sit movement. Unfortunately, to execute a back 3-turn, one must shift the weight to the heel of the blade. It is important to regain your balance by bending the skating knee to complete the turn and the exit edge. Repeat above in reverse for left foot.

Backward Inside 3-Turn. Start out on your left backward inside edge in the first position that was discussed for inside edges, executing the same movement as for the other 3-turns— push the hips against the shoulders. When you are on a left back inside edge, have both arms and shoulders turned to the left, outside of the curve you are skating. Your head is also looking to the left. Your right free leg is over the tracing.

To execute the turn, pull arms and shoulders across your hips, next you push the hips against the shoulders and arms, shifting the weight toward the heel of the left skating foot for the turn. Then, sit-lift-sit again as in all 3-turns.

The exit from this turn is made by turning to the outside of the circle, onto a left forward outside edge, with the right free leg remaining over the tracing for the entire turn. This final position is the second position, unlike the other 3-turns, which normally have three positions.

Mohawk Turn

The mohawk is a turn that goes from one direction to the other (forward to backward or backward to forward), and from one foot to the other. Although changing feet, you stay on the same edges (inside to inside or outside to outside).

The mohawk is one of the most common turns in skating and can be performed either forward or backward. To do a right forward inside mohawk, start off on the right inside edge, facing into the circle from the direction that you are traveling. The left free foot is held in a T-position, slightly inside but almost touching the instep of the skating foot.

Begin to turn the left free foot out as far to the left as you can; then transfer your weight from your right forward inside edge onto your left back inside edge. Your weight is transferred from the ball of the right foot to the ball of the left foot. Never have both feet on the ice at the same time.

As you turn, your arms and shoulders will turn naturally, followed by your hips and free foot. The arms are in an open position facing

RIGHT FORWARD INSIDE MOHAWK

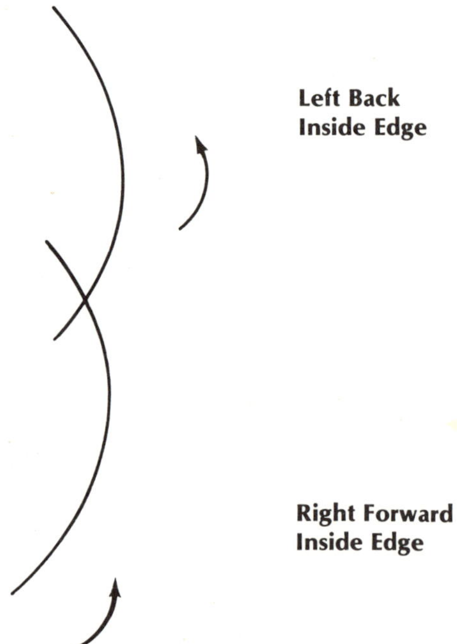

the inside of the circle. Or, another way of looking at it is—as you are traveling forward, the right arm and shoulder lead and the left arm is behind. After the turn, the right arm remains in the same position, which is now behind you, but the left arm is pressed across in front of the chest or perpendicular to the body.

When practicing this position, try to make each edge about three times your body height. Make a good strong curve. And learn to count six beats for each position, going forward and backward, to increase your balance and develop good edge control. Your aim is to skate the mohawk with a great amount of speed and control.

The right back outside mohawk is done by facing the outside of the circle as you are skating backward on a right back outside edge. Rotate your shoulders to the outside of the circle. The left free leg is in a T position, perpendicular to the instep of the right skating foot, as you skate to the left. To complete the maneuver, step down forward from the T position onto a left forward edge, with left arm in front and right free arm and leg extended in back.

If you use the mohawk for an entrance to a jump, *e.g.,* a waltz jump, you approach it from a right forward drop-mohawk position. This simply means that from your right back outside edge, you step into the left forward outside edge and continue into the takeoff for the jump. This drop mohawk will give a smooth flow to the approach and follow-through. As you are on the back edge, make certain that your shoulders are under control and are not swinging, or they will continue to swing on through the jump and over-rotate the body on the takeoff.

Choctaw Turn

A choctaw is another edge turn. You start from one direction and move to the other (forward to backward or backward to forward), changing feet as well as changing edges (*i.e.,* forward inside to backward outside or forward outside to backward inside).

CHOCTAW

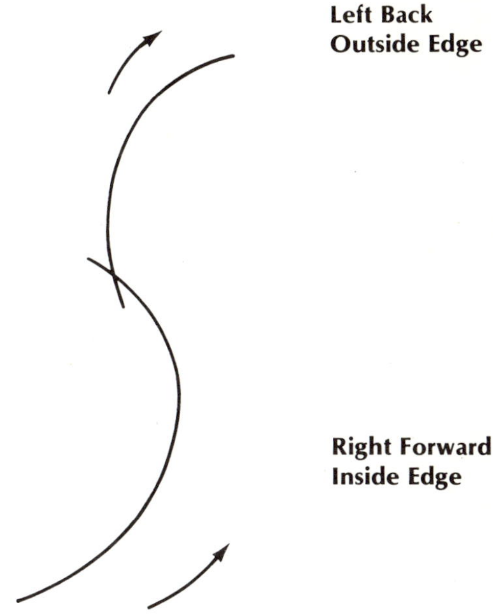

Skate a right forward inside edge. Bring the left free leg to the front of the body. Rotate the hips, shoulders, and arms toward the center of the circle, and, as you change direction, step down onto the left foot, placing the weight onto the left back outside edge. As you transfer your weight from one foot to the other, rotate arms, shoulders, and hips to the outside of the circle in the direction of your right free leg, which is extended behind.

There are many other more advanced turns such as brackets, counters, and rockers that should perhaps be at least mentioned. These are taught generally in the more advanced stages of figure skating especially in the areas of "patch" or "compulsory figure" tests and in the more advanced ice dance tests. It would take a lengthy chapter to explain each turn as each of these is executed both forward and backward as well as from outside and inside edges. In addition, by the time most skaters would be ready to handle these turns they would and should be taking regular skating lessons from a professional, well qualified in whatever field they are pursuing.

RIGHT FORWARD INSIDE CHOCTAW . . . stepping forward on a right inside edge **(left)**, your right arm is in front over the right skating leg with the shoulders and head rotating toward the center of the circle you are skating. The left free leg and foot are extended in front over the tracing. This movement resembles a letter "S" with the front right inside edge being the top part of the "S" and the stepping down onto a back left outside edge the bottom of the "S." You are skating the forward edge in one direction and reversing your direction by stepping down on a back left outside edge. In the second position **(right)**, the right free leg is extended in back over the tracing. Both arms and shoulders are checked severely to the right.

JUMPS

Freestyle skating requires the execution of various spins and jumps. These are connected by forward and backward turns, crossovers, and other skating maneuvers.

While most forward and backward skating moves will be performed on both the left and right edges, a skater usually favors one side or the other. That is, he has a strong side and a weak side, just as he might be right-handed or left-handed. It is good practice to be able to control yourself on all edges, from both the right and the left. But a skater will usually prefer jumping either to the right or to the left. If he can make a stronger and higher jump off the right leg, then that is the leg that all his jumps and spins will be practiced from. Choose the leg that you feel more confident on, and stick to that leg when executing all your jumps and spins.

As a general rule, right-handed skaters jump from left to right and rotate their spins to the left. Left-handed skaters do just the opposite. It is important that you are consistent. Otherwise, when you want to combine jumps and spins, as for a flying camel or flying sitspin, you will have great difficulty. You may have to relearn the jump or spin. The following jumps and spins are described as normally performed by a right-handed skater.

Waltz Jump

There are two types of jumps: edge jumps and toe jumps. For edge jumps, you take off from the edge of the blade, jumping slightly outside the curve of the circle, and landing again on the same curve from which you took off.

The waltz jump is the first jump most skaters learn. In a waltz jump, the skater takes off on a forward outside edge, rotates half a turn in the air, and lands on the back outside edge of the other foot.

From either backward crossovers or a mohawk (with the last position a right back outside edge with the right arm in line with the right skating leg and the left arm directly in back over the left free leg), step forward on the left forward outside edge, pressing your weight onto the ball of the left foot. At this point the right free leg is behind the body, your shoulders are parallel to your hips, and your arms are on either side of you. As you take off, bend your skating knee and transfer your weight forward to a point between the ball of your foot and the lowest toepick.

Having bent your skating knee and transferred your weight forward onto the left outside edge, jump into the air. As you leave the ice, use both of your arms and your free leg to help you rise by moving them forward and up. An important fact to remember in jumping is to always jump up to your highest point before rotating. At the peak of the jump, the arms pull into a balletic fifth position, with the fingers almost touching.

Rotate half a turn and prepare to land in a fully extended position on a right back outside edge, with the right, skating or landing knee bent. The left free leg is turned out and extended straight behind the body, slightly outside the landing edge, with toe pointed and your shoulders parallel over your hips with your head facing straight ahead.

When landing, also called *checking out,* you have to be in a strong "checkout position" before you make contact with the ice. Brace yourself. Do not let the hips, shoulders, or arms drop or move to the inside of the landing edge as you make contact with the ice, or over-rotation will result, causing you to lose control of the landing edge.

The landing position on the right back outside edge for the waltz jump is the same one you use before stepping forward for the waltz jump. The only difference in the two positions is that your left arm is extended in back over the left free leg in preparation for the takeoff, while the arms are parallel for the landing, or checkout, position. If the skater is having trouble controlling the landing, and is finding over-rotation a problem, this can be corrected by moving the left free arm slightly forward and in front of the body so that the left arm is perpendicular to the right arm. Most instructors prefer arms parallel for the landing, but others teach the landing with free arm forward. Both are correct.

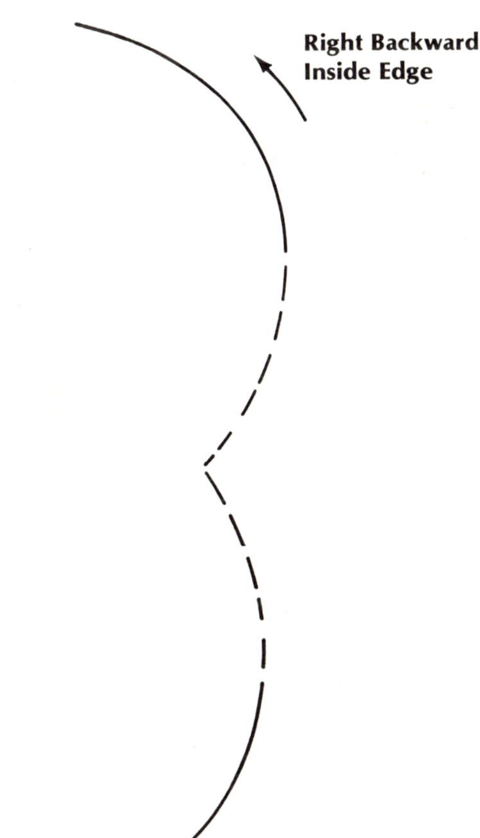

WALTZ JUMP (rotating to the left) . . . this waltz jump is taken from a right-handed jumping position. If you are left handed you will reverse the direction of the jump. Approaching from a mohawk and skating the right left outside edge **(left)**, step forward onto a left outside edge for the takeoff. The left skating knee is bent for the maximum amount of spring. The right free leg is over the tracing and both arms are at each side and slightly behind the body in preparation to swing forward in an upward direction together with the free leg for the takeoff. As you land **(right)**, your left free leg is extended behind you and both arms are extended to either side of the body. The skating knee is bent to absorb the landing.

Salchow

The salchow jump, named after former world champion Ulrich Salchow, consists of a full turn in the air from a back inside edge and a landing on the back outside edge of the other foot.

Approach this turn by first doing a left outside 3-turn. You will then be on a left back inside edge, with your shoulders in a strong checked position. From this position, the right free leg is rotated around the outside of the tracing until it is in front of the body and over the tracing in a slightly pigeon-toed position.

Continue the jump by bending the skating knee and springing into the air with your right arm leading and meeting the left arm. Your right free leg is making a forward circular motion.

As you are rising into the air, your arms move up to help you make the full revolution at the top of the jump. Then move the arms into a fifth position, in front of you at shoulder height; on landing, bring them into a checkout position. Remember never to rotate the shoulders before

you turn; always jump straight up. Jumping up, not around, will help you to find your center of gravity before you make the revolution.

As you finish a full revolution in the air, land on your right back outside edge in a strongly checked landing position, with arms out to either side of the body. The left free leg is extended behind you.

As in the waltz jump, don't begin turning in the air until you've reached the peak of your jump. The hips, as well as the shoulders, must not precede the body on takeoff, or you will be pulled off balance. What leaves the ice first is going to arrive first, which means that if your arms or hips leave the ice first, they will finish the revolution before your body. This will cause you to lose your balance and fall.

One of the most common errors is to leave the 3-turn for the takeoff before you have a controlled edge. If you are swinging about or falling off the edge as you prepare to go into the salchow jump, or have not made the proper check, you will not only be unsteady, but also will lose your balance. Even if you manage to

SALCHOW
(jumping to the left)

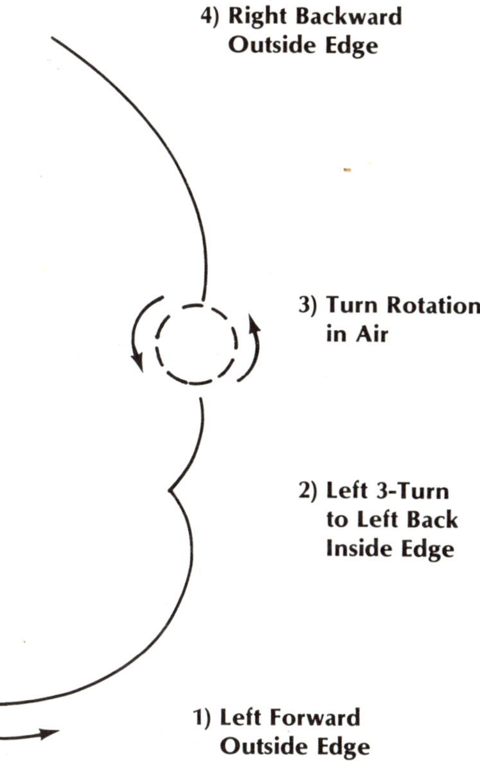

make the revolution in the air, you won't travel far from your takeoff point, and the jump will have little height. It will look like a spin!

You can increase your control of the jump by holding the back inside edge of the 3-turn as long as possible before takeoff. Try for distance on the jump. For a good jump, the landing will be at least three feet from the takeoff point. Make certain you don't fall off or lose control of that inside edge.

Loop Jump

For a loop jump, takeoff from a right back outside edge, making a full revolution in the air, and then landing backward on the same foot and the same back outside edge.

Enter the jump from either a right forward inside mohawk or a left forward outside 3-turn. Still remaining backward, step into your first position on a right back outside edge. The body, head, and shoulders will be facing toward the inside of the circle. Your left free foot will be

trailing on the ice in front of you, almost directly in line with your skating, or takeoff, foot. Press forward toward the ball of the takeoff foot and deepen the curve of the edge. If you do not deepen the curve or curl (a short, tight backward edge) before takeoff, it will be more difficult to make the rotation in the air.

You cannot execute the jump while taking off backward in a straight line. As you press forward for takeoff, and not a split second before, bring your right arm (not the shoulder) in to meet the left arm, which hasn't moved. As you are taking off, make sure your body stays square over the takeoff edge. Again, it is important not to let your hips or shoulders rotate before leaving the ice.

Your trailing left free foot is lifted just before takeoff, and continues squarely in front of the body until you prepare for landing. At the top of the jump, you tighten up the free leg, pull your arms in toward your chest, and make a full revolution in the air.

LOOP JUMP
(jumping to the left)

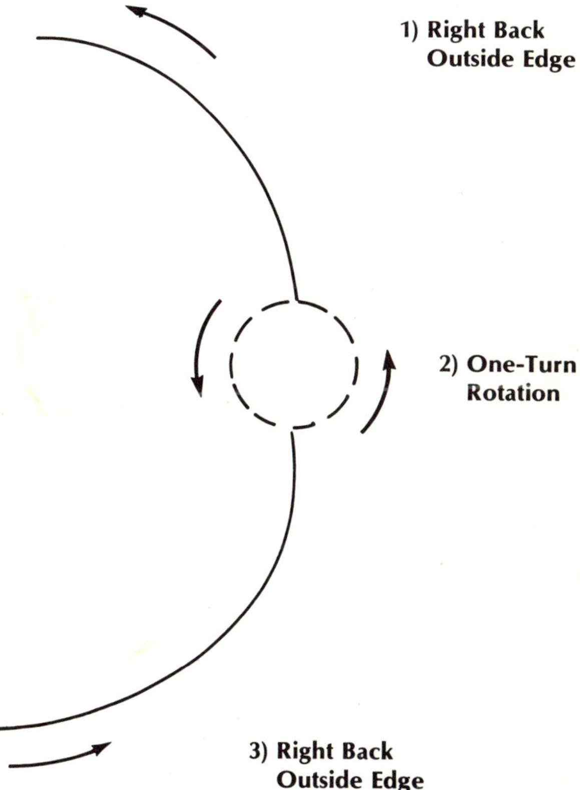

The right takeoff leg, which is now becoming the landing leg, prepares for landing. As you are descending, you move the left free leg back to the rear of the skating leg to a full checkout position, with your arms extended out to your sides and your left free leg extended in back and slightly outside the landing edge.

Most errors are made in loop jumps by letting the left free leg swing outside the tracing instead of remaining in front of the takeoff foot before the jump. Do not let the shoulders rotate before the jump. Keep your body and hips squarely over the edge when taking off. All these factors are important for balance on takeoff and during the jump itself.

Falling-Leaf Jump

The falling-leaf jump can be beautiful if executed properly. The skater begins the takeoff preparation in the same manner as for a loop jump: skating backward from back crossovers; taking off from right back outside edge; and turning toward the outside of the circle.

The left free leg, however, makes a different movement than it does for the loop jump. The leg swings forward and extends in the direction you are rotating. Make a half-revolution in the air, landing forward on the toepick of the left foot. Follow immediately with a strong, right forward inside edge. The arms are extended out to the sides.

Split Falling-Leaf Jump. The split falling-leaf is the same as the falling-leaf jump, except it requires, at the peak of the jump, a perfect split position, with the left leg leading in the direction you are turning. The right leg remains in back, toes pointed and legs turned out. The left arm is directly over the left leg, and the right arm is in back over the right leg. Landing is on the left toepick and right inside edge.

Toe Loop Jump

The toe loop jump is generally a skater's introduction to toe jumping. For this jump, take off from a slight curved edge and with the assistance of the toepick of the free foot.

Approach a toe loop jump on a left forward inside edge with your right free leg extended in front of the body. Make a right inside 3-turn and, after completing the turn, extend the left free leg straight behind, in line with the curve of the edge you are skating. In all toepick jumps, the toe of the free leg is placed behind the skating foot, directly in line with the body.

The toepick of the left free foot is placed on the ice with the toe pointing downward. This keeps the toepicks from sliding out from under-

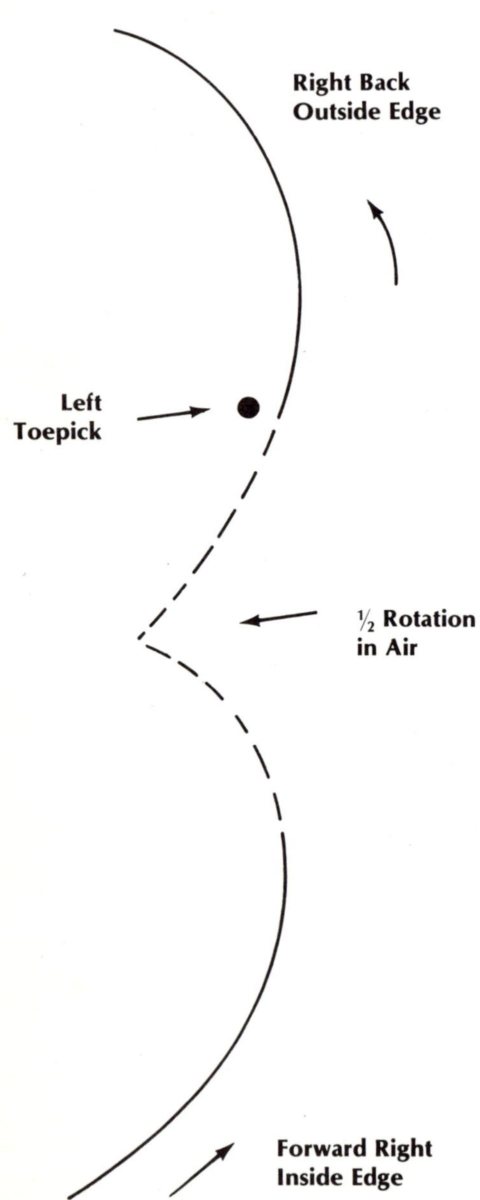

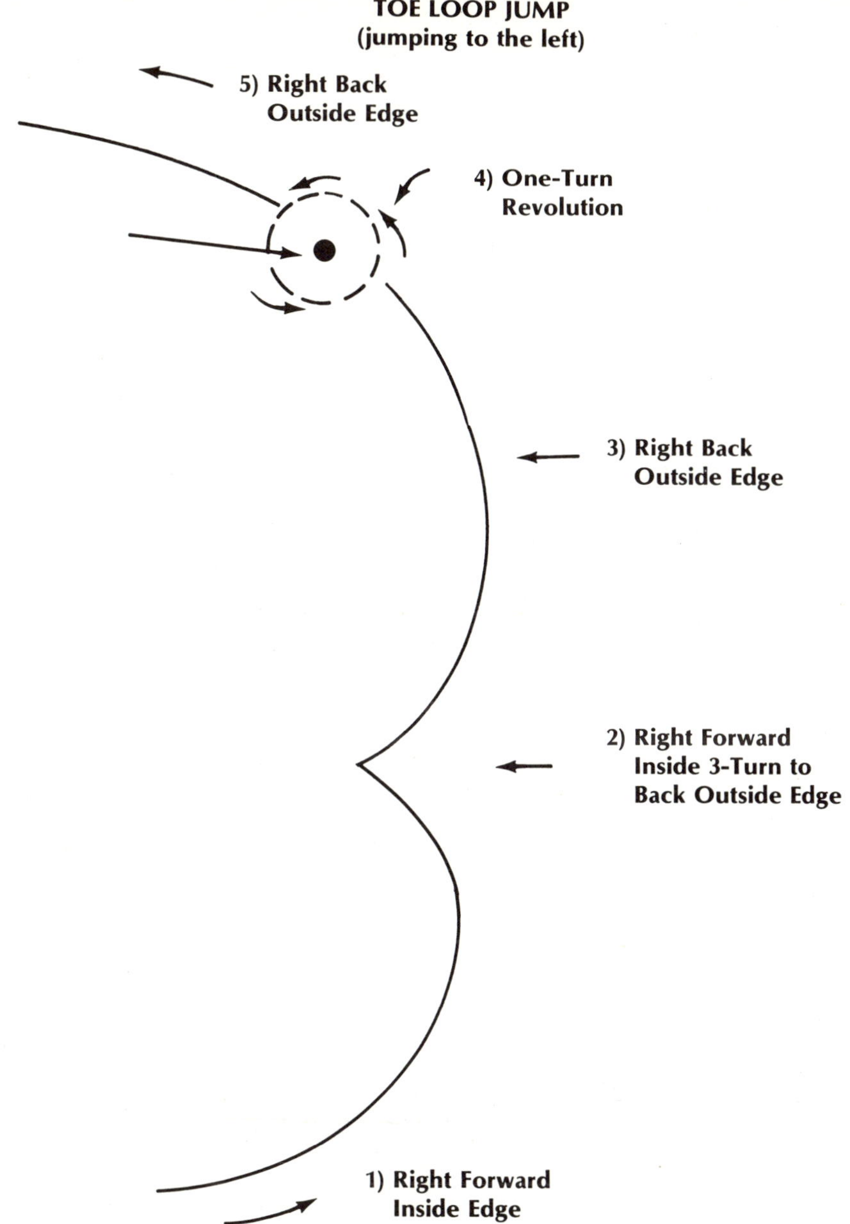

neath you as you take off. For this to take place, your hips must be parallel to each other and at a right angle to the tracing.

In preparation for the takeoff, bend your skating knee and place your left arm in front of you in line with your left shoulder. Your right arm is at a right angle to your body. Begin the takeoff by drawing your right skating foot toward the toepick and springing into the air. As soon as you have put the toepick of the left foot into the ice and you are in the air, use the right free leg in the same manner that you did for the waltz jump. As you are leaving the ice, your right arm moves to meet the left arm, which has remained in front of the body. The arms proceed to the familiar fifth position, and, as you reach the top of the jump, they pull in toward the chest.

When descending, bring the left free leg through to the back of the skating leg in a full, extended checked position, with the arms at shoulder height at either side of the body.

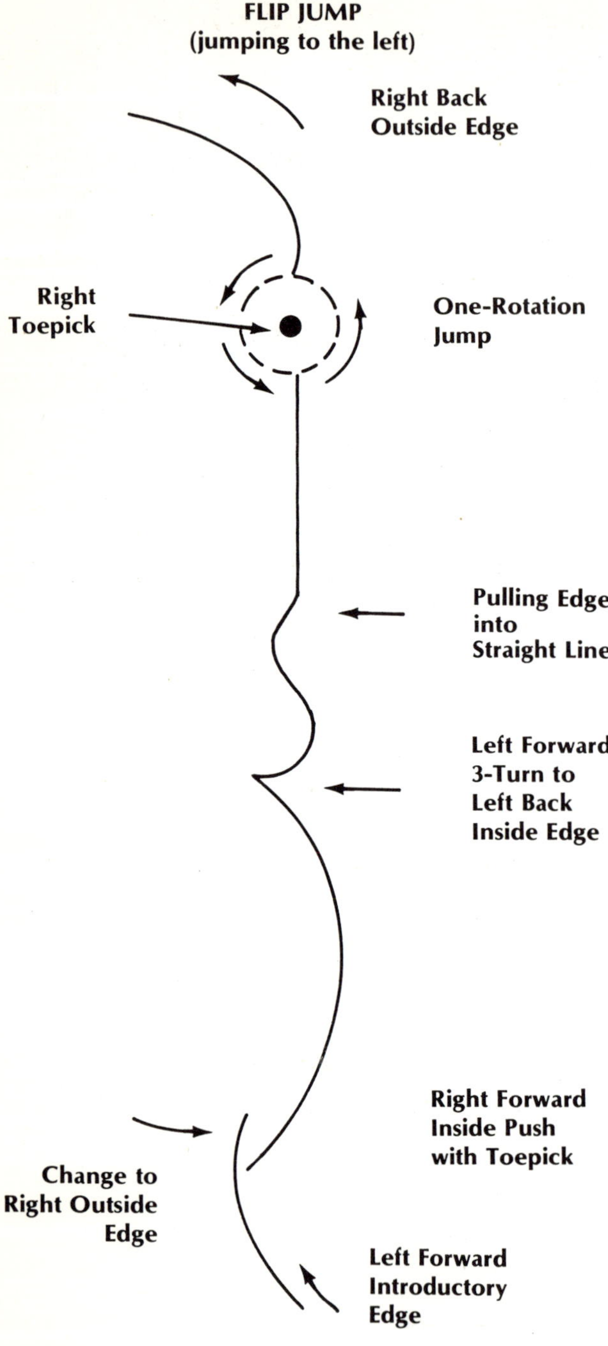

Flip Jump

The flip jump is approached from a shallow left forward inside edge, with the right skating foot extended directly in front of the body. Use the right free foot to direct you into a left forward outside 3-turn, drawing or pulling the back edge of this turn down the ice into a straight line. This takeoff position requires much practice. Drawing a 3-turn into a straight line takes a great deal of control.

As you bend your left skating knee for the takeoff, extend your right free leg straight backward in line with your body. Face the pick of the free foot straight down into the ice. Your left arm is extended to the front, in line with your body. The right arm is directly behind you.

Don't rotate your shoulders or hips before taking off. Begin the takeoff by drawing the left skating foot toward your right toepick foot, while springing into the air. As you rise, move your right arm to meet your left arm, which is still in front. Begin rotating and pull the arms into fifth position and then into the chest. During the jump, both legs are parallel and close together directly under the body.

Complete the jump (one full revolution in the air) and bring the left free leg through and back into a fully extended checkout position.

Lutz Jump

The lutz jump is the first reverse jump (counterclockwise) that you will do. Approach it from right-over-left backward crossovers on a very large semicircle.

Enter this jump on a left backward outside edge and draw it into a straight line with your right free foot extended in front of you. The left arm is also extended in front of the body in line with your left shoulder. Your right arm is in back, following the same line and at the same height as the right shoulder. The opposite arm and leg are extended in front (left arm and right free leg). This is the first position for the lutz jump.

For the second position, move the right free leg directly behind you. Bend your skating knee in preparation for the takeoff, making certain that arms and shoulders have not moved from the first position. When you bend the skating knee, place the toe of the free foot, or picking foot, directly down and into the ice behind you in a straight line. Draw the skating foot back toward the toepick foot.

Don't place the toepick foot to the outside, instead of directly behind you, or you will slide off the pick. A similar problem arises if you cross the toepick foot too far behind, causing the hips and shoulders to precede the rest of the body before the takeoff. This causes an already prerotated jump and results in a severe lean.

LUTZ JUMP . . . after approaching the lutz jump **(left)** with the right free foot extended in front, right arm behind in line with the body, and left arm in front of you, take off from a left back outside edge, placing the right toepick directly behind the body with the left arm still in front and the right arm in back. The head is forward. In the air, as you make one revolution, the arms pull in toward the chest and the legs are extended straight downward underneath the body **(right)**. Execute the landing in the normal checkout position on the right back outside edge.

LUTZ JUMP
(jumping to the left)

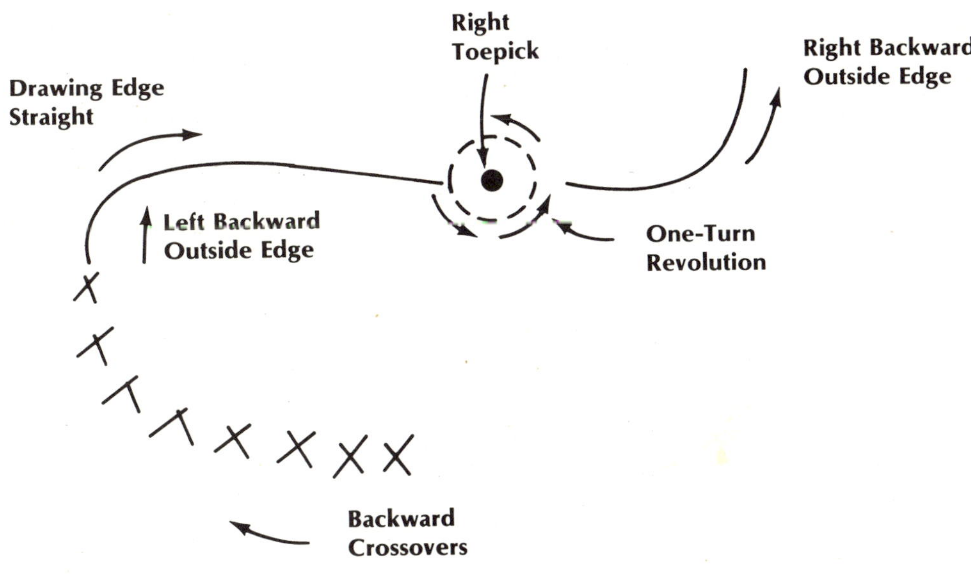

When you place the toepick foot into the ice behind you, check to make sure your shoulders remain in the same position, and then proceed with the takeoff, remembering to draw the jump backward in the direction you are traveling. Then, jump straight up into the air.

After the takeoff, move your right arm in to meet your left arm. As you rotate in the air, pull the arms inward toward the chest, making one revolution as you pass the left free leg through to the back, into a checkout landing position. The arms also move to a fully extended checkout position.

In both the flip jump and the lutz jump, the main thing to remember is to draw the body backward in a straight line toward the toepick foot, and then jump straight up in the air. Do not break at the waist or lean forward.

Axel Jump

An axel jump, named after Axel Paulsen, is the first jump that a skater attempts that requires more than one full revolution in the air.

If you've had no qualified instruction up until now on the various jumps and maneuvers we've discussed, now is the time to find a good teacher. An axel jump is too difficult to learn without guidance. Many mistakes can be made, and once bad habits are developed, they can take a long time to break. Your teacher will be your mirror or eyes to help you see what you are doing when you are rotating high in the air.

The axel consists of 1½ revolutions in the air, after takeoff from a left forward outside edge, and a landing backward on the right back outside edge.

The approach for the axel is the same as for the waltz jump—from either a right forward inside mohawk or from right backward crossovers or left foot crossing over right—placing you on the curve of a large semicircle on a right backward outside edge. The right skating knee is bent; your hips are square over the tracing; your right arm and shoulder are directly in line with your right skating leg; and your left arm and shoulder are in line with your left free leg. The free leg is extended behind your body with the toe pointed and turned out.

If this position is performed correctly, you shouldn't have to make any adjustments of the body as you step forward onto the left forward outside edge for the takeoff. There should be only a slight increase in backward pressure by both arms for the takeoff and the change of the feet.

Starting your spring from the left outside edge, push off from the ice by straightening the skating knee and rolling forward—on the left outside edge—toward the toe of the skating foot. At the same time you are shifting your weight forward, swing both arms from behind, closely past the body, and forward and upward. Your right free leg coincides with your arms, moving forward and up. The knee of the right free leg is slightly bent as it swings upward into the air.

The rotation dictates the height of the jump. The jump will continue to rise only as long as you delay rotation. Jump straight up into the air and reach the peak before you start the rotation. At the peak of the jump, your body must be straight, with your legs underneath you, as if suspended from the ceiling by the head. The rotation is created by drawing the arms toward the chest and closing the free leg in and down to the skating leg.

As you begin the descent, transfer your weight from the left takeoff leg to the right free leg, which is to become the landing leg. Obtain the checkout position by moving your arms out into the landing position and at the same time bringing your left free leg through toward the back of the body. Your weight has now shifted completely from your left takeoff foot to your right foot, which is now your landing foot. The left foot and leg are now in a checkout position behind the body, slightly outside the curve of the landing edge. The arms are out to the sides.

Split Jump

Before attempting a split jump, you should know how to do a half flip jump, landing forward on the left toepick and the forward inside edge of the right foot.

The most common entrance is from a right forward mohawk into a straight line down the ice. From this point, use the same preparation

AXEL (rotating to the left) . . . start on a left forward outside edge in preparation for the takeoff with both arms and free leg extended behind the body. As you prepare for the jump **(left)**, the right free leg starts to pass through to the front as both arms and free leg simultaneously move forward and up. At the peak of the jump **(center)**, the free leg is bent and the arms are pulled in toward the chest. The body is directly over the left jumping leg. As you start descending **(right)**, the arms are moving downward toward the waist in preparation for the landing. Check out in regular landing position on a back right outside edge as demonstrated in the waltz jump.

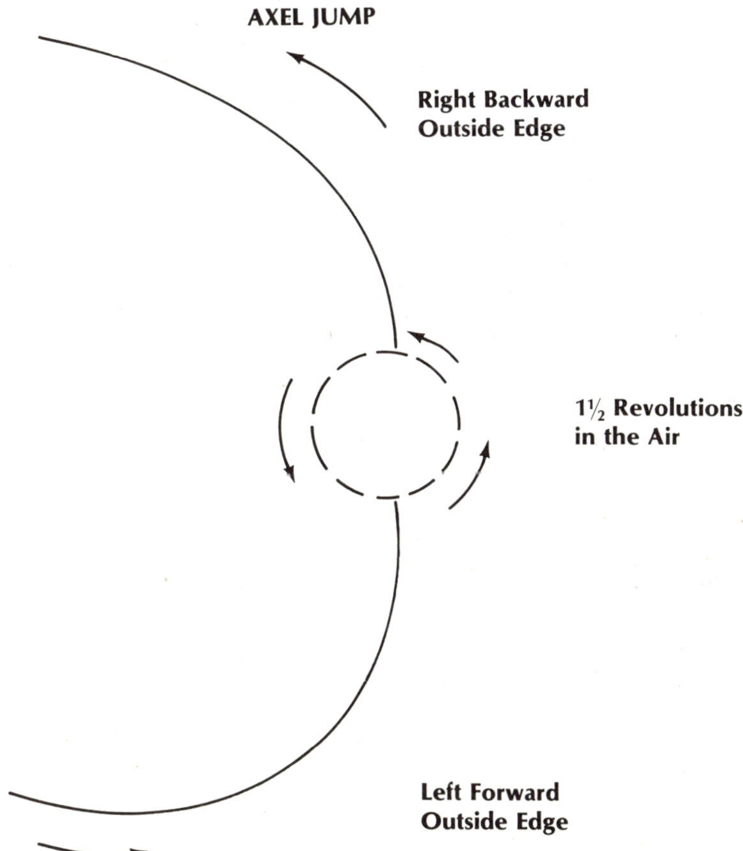

SPLIT JUMP . . . a split jump is usually entered from a forward mohawk. Upon completing the mohawk and preparing for the takeoff **(top),** extend the left free leg and toepick directly behind you as far as possible. The skating leg is strongly bent and your left free leg must be straight as you place the toepicks into the ice. The arms and shoulders are in a checked position with the right arm over the right skating leg and the left arm over the left free leg. Spring into the air and turn the body forward to the front with the right free leg, toe and hips extended in a turned out, or open, position. The right arm is directly over the right leg. The left leg remains behind in an open position with the left arm extended over the left leg. This fully-extended split jump **(bottom),** was demonstrated during a performance. It is being executed by a left-handed skater, rotating to the right. Please reverse for the right-handed skater, rotating to the left.

as for the flip jump—placing the left arm in front of the body at shoulder height and the right arm behind you in line with the front arm. Extend the right free leg in a straight line directly behind the body. Shoulders and hips are checked and ready for the takeoff. The toepick is placed downward, into the ice, and you spring up into the air, jumping from a strongly bent left skating knee, assisted by the right toepick. Maintaining a checked position with the arms and hips, rotate the body ½ revolution and land forward on your left toepick. The right inside edge follows immediately.

At the peak of the jump, split the legs, with the left leg in front toward the direction you are traveling. The right leg is behind. The legs and knees are open and turned out and straight with the toes pointed and also turned out. The left arm is in front at shoulder height, directly over the left leg, and the right arm is in back, directly over the right leg.

A succession of split jumps can be done by following each with a right inside mohawk and taking off immediately for another jump.

SPINS

As with jumps, spins are usually performed in

one direction only—the direction of the jump. If you jump to the left, you spin to the left, and vice versa.

In competitive skating, some jumps and spins are executed in both directions. This is very difficult to do and is usually done to achieve extra points for difficulty factor from the judges. This, however, is not necessary, and most skaters spin and jump in only one direction.

There are three types of spins from which variations are derived: the upright, or one foot spin; the sit spin; and the camel spin.

Centering a Spin

The most important thing to learn about spinning is how to center a spin correctly. Centering a spin means placing one's spin in the center of a circle and staying there. This enables you to execute a spin with a great deal of speed and prolong the rotation so that it seems to "last forever." An uncentered spin will travel, or move off one particular spot, preventing the skater from increasing the speed of the spin without loss of balance. It also prevents a skater from holding the position of the spin for any length of time.

In learning how to center the spin, approach the spin by doing two or three right outside backward crossovers around a small circle in a clockwise direction. The last crossover places you on a right back inside edge as you prepare to step into the center of the circle you have just made. While on the back inside edge, rotate your arms and shoulders to the outside of the circle. Your left free leg is extended behind you in line with your spine. From this right back inside edge, step into the center of your circle, placing the weight of your left foot on a strong, left forward outside edge. Maintain a deeply bent knee with the left skating leg. This left forward outside edge points in the opposite direction of the right back inside edge. As you step onto this edge, lead with your left arm and shoulder. Hook, or loop, a small circle with your left foot by skating a left 3-turn at the end of this sharp, hooked left edge, and then spin on a back inside edge directly over the 3-turn. Your right free leg starts to swing around to the outside of the small circle you are creating,

moving forward and remaining on the right side of the body at approximately the same height as the knee of your left spinning leg. Arms have moved to each side of the body at shoulder height, and the hips remain squarely over the tracing. Your weight has now shifted toward the ball of the foot, just under the lowest toepick. Your legs are like a compass, used to scribe a circle, with your left, or centering, leg as the pivot point and your right free leg swinging to the outside, creating the spin. Remain at this balancing point for a second to make certain that your body is balanced and in line. You are now rotating in one spot.

Once centered, begin to increase the speed of the spin by pulling against the centrifugal force. By pulling your arms and free leg against this force, you create an increase in speed. Move your arms in, first bringing them from the sides of the body to the front in fifth position, with your arms rounded and at shoulder level. Grab your hands, interlacing your fingers, and pull them toward your chest. At the same time your hands and arms move in toward your chest, your free leg has drawn in from the knee to whatever position coincides with the spin you are executing. Arms remain at shoulder level.

With your hands next to your chest, you have completed the spin. Prepare to slow down and exit on a backward right outside edge with left free leg extended straight behind you.

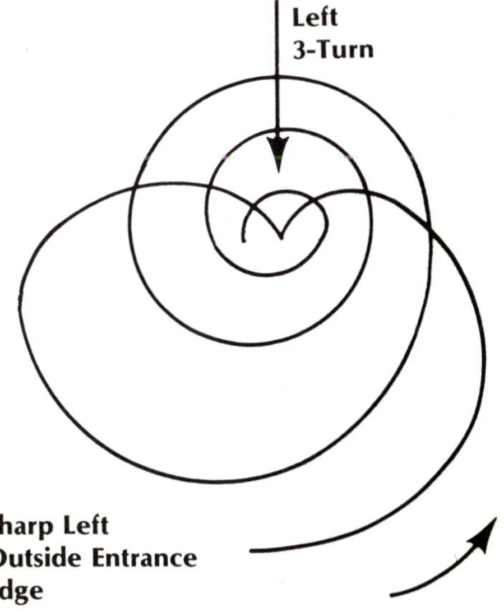

CENTERING A SPIN
(spinning to the left)

TWO-FOOT SPIN (rotating to the left) . . . after stepping into the circle and centering your spin, place your feet and legs parallel to each other with the toes slightly pigeon-toed. Your arms and hands are extended in front with the hands almost touching. To increase your speed, draw the arms in as if hugging a beach ball.

Two-Foot Spin

Repeat the preparation for centering a spin from backward crossovers. Stepping into the center of the circle, bring the right free leg around to your right side, with your arms extended to the sides of the body at shoulder height. This time the free leg is drawn down toward the ice and is placed next to the spinning foot, distributing the weight equally between the two legs, with the feet slightly apart.

This spin is easier to execute by keeping the toes pointed slightly inward or pigeon-toed. Your knees are bent and your head is facing directly ahead—not moving in the direction of the spin—to complete your first position.

Increase the speed of the spin by using the same method we discussed earlier—bringing your arms and hands in front toward each other, with arms rounded at approximately shoulder height, for the second position of the spin.

The third position is created when you pull against the centrifugal force and increase the speed of the spin. The hands meet in front of the body, the fingers interlace, and you pull toward the chest, keeping your arms at shoulder level. This movement is similar to hugging a beachball.

Upon completion of the spin, exit by using the left foot to push out onto a right backward outside edge, with arms on either side of the body. The free leg is extended in back in the same checkout position executed when landing after a jump.

One-Foot Spin

Draw a circle by skating backward crossovers and stepping into the center in the same manner as for the two foot spin. Place your body in the first position with your right free leg out to the side and arms at shoulder height on each side of the body. Move into a second position by bringing the hands to the front of the body in fifth position, with the arms rounded and again at shoulder height.

Your weight is forward on the blade, just under the toepick that is closest to the ball of the spinning foot. You actually use the ball of the foot as well as the bottom toepick when doing a one foot spin.

Through the entire spin, your skating knee should be slightly bent for balance and pressure on the ice. Some teachers have a pupil momentarily rise up onto a straight left skating leg before settling onto a bent skating knee. This must be done with great care because too stiff a knee can cause the skater to rise too much, thereby losing spinning pressure on the ice.

The third position is the drawing inward of the hands in front of the body with the arms rounded at shoulder height. The third position is different than for the two foot spin: at the same time that you draw your arms and hands

ONE-FOOT SPIN (rotating to the left) . . . in the first position **(left)** of a one-foot spin the right leg is extended to the side. The arms are shoulder high on either side of the body. The head is facing straight ahead. In the second position **(right)** the free leg is brought in to touch the knee.

toward the chest, bring your right free leg in toward your left spinning leg, bending it from the knee, but keeping the hips level at all times. The right foot of the free leg rests next to, or touching, the inside of the left skating knee for the remainder of the spin. The arms are drawn inward next to the chest.

As the spin slows down, prepare to exit by bending your elbows down alongside the body, bringing your hands down to chest level, and pushing out onto the right backward outside edge.

Scratch Toe, or Blur Spin

The scratch toe spin is executed in much the same way as a one foot spin, by duplicating the first and second positions. The exception comes with the second position: the free leg does not remain to the side of the body. As the arms round and the hands join in front, the right free leg moves to the front and is positioned under the center of the fifth position the arms have

made (a slight open circle).

The third position is made by drawing the hands and right free leg in toward the body at exactly the same time and, most importantly, at the same rate of speed. The right free leg has remained at a height slightly above that of the left skating knee, and any raising or lowering of the free leg at any time throughout the spin will throw the spin off balance and cause the skater to travel, losing speed and possibly the spin.

If you can place the right foot above the left knee, all the better: the higher the free foot on the skating leg, the longer the spin. The only movement that should happen as you bend the right knee and pull the right foot inward should be from the right knee down to the right foot. The finish of the third position should find the skater with arms in front of the chest, the right knee bent, the right free foot turned out and across (or above) the left spinning leg, and the hips and shoulders level.

Clasping hands or lacing fingers gives the skater more control, especially in a scratch toe

BLUR SPIN OR SCRATCH TOE SPIN

(rotating to the left) . . . stepping into a scratch toe spin (the same as for a one-foot spin) **(top left)** maintain your first position with the arms extended shoulder high, but the right free leg is extended more toward the front than to the side in a one-foot spin.

In the second position **(above)** the arms are drawn in toward the chest at the same time you bring the free leg and foot in to touch the skating knee. Note that the free foot is turned out, touching and crossing in front of the skating knee.

The third position **(left)** occurs when you start to increase the speed by simultaneously starting to move both arms up and directly over your head. At the same time, draw the right free leg in front toward the ice still maintaining the crossed position in front of the skating leg. Clasp your hands and interlace the fingers to prevent the arms from flying out causing loss of control.

spin. It keeps the arms from flying out, creating a loss of control.

The fourth and final position is tight with a rigid body line. From the third position, you start to draw the right free leg down across the front of your skating leg until the ankle of the right free leg is tightly across the ankle of the left skating leg. The heel of the right free leg is pressed downward, toward the ice. As you draw the free leg downward and across the skating leg, you move the arms upward until they are fully extended over the head, with the fingers still tightly clasped. You should be at your maximum rate of speed at this point—ideally, a blur on the ice.

The body weight is between the ball of the skating foot and the bottom toepick. Push your weight into the ice, creating a pressure similar to a drill. In this final position, your arms and free leg are drawn upward and downward respectively. Simultaneously, the skating leg straightens, and the body, arms, and legs become rigid, creating the drill feeling. If at this point you do not maintain the downward pressure into the ice, you can actually snap yourself off your spinning foot.

Change Foot Spin

The change foot spin is exactly that—a change from one foot to the other and back to the original foot.

To start this spin, begin by doing a one foot spin. Spin on your left foot with the right free leg extended to the side. Next, the right foot moves downward toward the left spinning foot until it replaces the spinning foot. The transfer of weight from one foot to the other is done smoothly and quickly. Pick up your left foot and tuck it next to the knee of your right skating leg. The arms are still out to the side of the body, at shoulder height, in the open position.

Although you have changed feet, you are still spinning in the same direction, but now on a right backward outside edge. (Some professionals teach it as a right forward inside edge.) Spin on this new skating leg at least three to five revolutions. Then transfer back to your original foot for the final spin, this time with your right free foot extended to the side. Draw your arms and free leg in toward your chest to finish the spin. If you pull your arms in toward your chest before the final spin, there will be no way to increase your speed for the final rotations.

Although the change foot spin is not very popular, it is helpful when teaching the skater how to spin backward on the foot that he seldom uses for spins. In other words, it teaches a person who is accustomed to spinning on the left foot how to spin backward on the right foot or do a reverse spin. This is necessary for spins such as the flying camel spin, sit change sit, camel jump camel, and other combination spins that involve changing feet.

Sit Spin

The sit spin is easily identifiable. While good skaters perform this move "effortlessly," don't underestimate the amount of practice that it requires.

Before trying to spin in this position, try to position yourself while standing still. Hold onto the railing of your skating rink and try to sit as low over the skating foot as possible with your chest over your knees and your weight on the ball of your skating foot.

Enter a one foot spin with the usual back-crossover preparation. As you step onto your left foot, center your spin. Your right free leg swings around the right side of the body in an arc until it reaches the front. As the free leg is making the swing, shift your weight over the ball of your left spinning foot and start to sink into the sitting position.

The farther you descend, the more your weight must shift toward the front of the skating blade, until you are in the final sit spin position. If you sit too low, you'll rock back onto the heel of the spinning foot and lose your balance. Ideally, your derriere should be lower than the skating knee and line or lower than the top of the boot of the same foot. The heel of the skating blade should be slightly off the ice. You will be spinning between the ball of the foot and the toepick that is closest to the ball of the foot.

The free leg is now in front of the body, extended straight out, with the knee and toe turned out in an open position. The thigh and

SIT SPIN . . . entrance is a strong forward outside edge. The body is upright with the arms out to the side. The right free leg swings around the side to the front (spinning to the left). As you start down into a sitting position, the weight shifts forward over the ball of the spinning foot (**front and side view**).

knee of the right free leg are hugging tightly to the thigh and knee of the left skating thigh and knee. The heel is facing upward and the toe is pointed downward. The back is straight and the head is facing forward.

The left hand rests on your left skating knee, and your right arm and hand should be extended over your right free leg. A variation is to have both arms and hands extended over the free leg.

To maintain your balance, you must keep your weight forward, but without dropping onto an outside or deep inside edge or you'll lose the center of the spin.

Rising to get out of the sit spin is difficult. You have to pitch yourself forward and up with a straight back. This movement resembles trying to get out of a tiny baby chair.

The momentum for the sit spin comes from the initial push onto the entrance edge and the swing forward and around the right free leg as you prepare to go down into the sit position. Momentum is increased by drawing the right free leg in toward the left spinning leg. Don't wrap it around the spinning leg, as this looks unattractive. After much practice, you should be able to spin on a dime.

Camel Spin

The camel spin comes from a ballet movement called the arabesque (in skating terms known as a spiral). It is performed by executing the usual backward crossovers and stepping forward onto the left forward outside edge. The body position, though, is different from that for any of the other spins you have previously learned.

The entrance to the spin is on a strong, forward outside edge, but the body is already in a spiral position with the right free leg extended high in back, in line with the spine. The toe of the right free leg is turned out and pointed, and held higher than the heel. The skating knee is severely bent. The left skating arm is forward and the right arm is extended back over the right free leg.

As you enter the spin, the rotation is created by simultaneously straightening the skating knee, pulling back on the left arm and shoulder until they are parallel to the right arm and shoulder, arching the back, and lifting the head and chin. This is all executed in one smooth movement. A sudden jerk will cause a sideways pitch that will pull you out of your spin.

CAMEL SPIN . . . entrance edge for the camel spin is on a deep left forward outside edge **(left)**. The right free leg is in back, the skating knee bent, and the arms out to the sides. Straighten the left leg **(right)** and skating knee, arch the back, pull the shoulders and arms backward and up. The weight shifts toward the middle of the blade.

Throughout the entire entrance and spin, the hips remain at right angles to the tracing and parallel to the shoulders.

It is important to note that as you straighten the knee of the spinning leg, you must compensate by pushing the weight to the heel of that blade. While continuing to spin, equalize your balance and weight along the entire blade that is spinning on a left forward outside edge. Your arms are on either side of your body, slightly behind, creating a graceful line that compliments the arch of the back.

To exit from this spin, straighten your body up to a one foot spin position with the right free leg out to the right side. Your arms are on both sides, in line with the shoulders, as you complete the spin.

Flying Camel Spin

When you can confidently perform a change foot spin and a forward camel, you'll be ready to move on to a flying camel spin.

The flying camel takes off from a very strong outside edge, but is not followed by a spin at this point (unlike the camel spin); rather, it is followed by a jump. You jump from one foot to the other—taking off forward and landing backward—into a backward spin, as if you were doing a waltz jump and landing in a backward spin.

From the same spiral takeoff position used for a forward camel, you create an arc by jumping around yourself and landing backward on the other foot, outside the arc or edge you just created, spinning in a right backward camel position. As you land, your right skating knee is bent to absorb the shock. Your arms are out to the sides, pressed slightly back and up. Your back is arched, and your head and chin are up. Immediately straighten the spinning leg and knee, and distribute your weight evenly over the entire blade of the new spinning foot. After jumping, the momentum of the backward camel is sustained upon landing by the sudden yet smooth straightening of the right landing leg, along with the arching and lifting of the back, head, and arms.

Make certain the left free leg is already behind you before you land in the right backward camel spin. If it isn't, you'll lose the momentum of the spin or you'll fall onto too deep an outside edge, losing the spin this way, too.

LAYBACK SPIN . . . the body leans backward with the weight of the left spinning foot forward onto the ball of the foot **(left)**. The free leg is behind you (spinning to the left). Spinning on small back inside circles **(right)**, spin to the right.

The Layback Spin

The layback spin starts out in an upright position, the same as for a one foot spin. The arms are in the first position, out to the sides at shoulder height, with right free leg extended out to the side.

For the second position, the right free leg moves back, with the arms open and the palms of the hands facing the ceiling, even with the shoulders.

In the third position, the free leg lifts into as high an attitude position as possible, behind the body, with the knee and toe turned out. As you begin to place the free leg in the attitude position, start to lean the body backward. But before this backward lean occurs, make certain that you have centered your spin and that your hips are at right angles to the tracing. If your free leg is out to the side, don't continue the spin or your balance will be off.

Continue to lay back and push your hips and pelvis directly forward to counter the weight of the head and shoulders dropping back. The farther you lay back, the more the pelvis and hips must compensate. The weight shifts forward to the toepick closest to the ball of the skating foot. Maintain the spin in the layback position for as long as possible.

To exit, pull upright into a one foot spin, with the right free leg extended back out to the side. The arms are in an open position. Continue to bring the arms and free leg in to complete the spin.

SPREAD EAGLES

There are two types of spread eagles: the

FORWARD OUTSIDE SPREAD EAGLE
. . . is executed by skating forward in a large circle and maintaining a right outside edge. Your legs are in an open position with the left foot also dropping onto a left outside edge. The right foot is in front of the body and the left foot behind. The hips are parallel and the pelvis is pressed forward. The left arm and shoulder are pressed slightly to the right to help hold you on the curve of the circle.

FORWARD INSIDE SPREAD EAGLE . . .
Your right foot leads and your left foot trails onto the same curve. Lean forward from the blade into the curve you are skating.

BAUER . . . traveling forward the right leg is extended in front with knee extremely bent and right foot on a forward inside edge. Left leg extended straight out in back also on an inside edge. Hips are pressed forward, back arched, and weight divided between both legs.

forward outside and the forward inside. *The forward outside spread eagle* is easily learned by skating forward and stepping onto a right forward outside edge. As you step onto this edge, swing the left free leg forward to the front, with the toe turned out. Then immediately swing it to the back and place it on the outside edge, directly in line with the right skating leg. The left trailing foot will be slightly in front of the tracing of the right front foot, thereby making it easier to skate a deeply curved outside edge. Once in the spread eagle position, use your shoulders and arms to apply pressure in the direction you are skating (the right). Your hips and pelvis are pressed forward, your knees are straight, and you are leaning as far back as possible into the curve you are creating. The skater should try spread eagles in both directions to find out which he or she prefers.

You approach the *forward inside spread eagle* in the same manner as the outside spread eagle, except you are on inside edges. Your right foot leads and your left foot trails on the same curve. Lean forward, away from the blade, into the curve you are skating.

BAUER

Enter the bauer the same way you would a spread eagle, but bend the front knee to an extreme position, placing your body weight forward. Keep the back straight.

The free leg is extended behind you, and both the front and back feet are on inside edges with your weight divided between the extremely bent, right front leg and the straight, left back leg. Press the hips as far forward as possible and drop your body and head as far backward as possible. Usually the opposite shoulder and arm of the skating leg are pressed forward to prevent rotation and to help maintain a straight line. The other arm is extended to the side, perpendicular to the body.

8
Pair Skating

In pair skating, two partners perform movements in unison, giving the impression of total "togetherness." All types of free-skating movements, such as lifts, spins, spirals and spread eagles, are permissible, as long as the movements of skaters have a common resemblance.

Pair skating differs from ice dancing in that while the pair concentrates on complex turns, spins, and lifts, ice dancers are more synonymous with footwork and edging sequences. Pair skating has more lifts and jumps than ice dancing. And in ice dancing, lifts must be kept level with the man's waist. Basic rules for ice dancing will be discussed in the next chapter.

Pair skating competitions are divided into two categories: short programs and long programs. The short program requires pairs to perform six compulsory maneuvers, with connecting steps, not exceeding two minutes in duration. The sequence of required maneuvers is optional, and the program can be skated to music of the couple's choice.

Many rules govern pair-skating competitions. The rules are listed in the *United States Figure Skating Association Rule Book.*

Pair skating requires teamwork. Size is important in pair skating: the man must be taller and heavier than the woman. The pair must also be matched in ability and appearance. Each skater must learn to understand and relate to his partner's movements and abilities. He must be able to anticipate the other's moves and match each movement or step with precision. The couple should move and breathe as one, giving a unified appearance on the ice.

Pair skating is an advanced branch of figure skating and should be tried only by strong, skilled skaters. Many of the maneuvers are done at high speeds, with skaters only inches apart and blades crossing each other on the ice. Needless to say, inexperienced skaters could be badly hurt if they didn't know what they were doing.

WALTZ POSITION

While Samuel Pepys danced on the ice with Nell Gwynn in London in 1683, pair skating did not fully blossom until 200 years later. The

waltz position was the first form of organized pair skating.

The waltz position is also known as the closed position. For this position, the man and woman face each other with one partner skating forward and the other skating backward.

The man's right hand is placed firmly between the woman's shoulder blades. The woman's left hand rests firmly on a spot a little below her partner's right shoulder. Her left elbow rests on his right elbow. The man's left arm and the woman's right arm are extended to the side at shoulder height and are held firmly to insure synchronized movement.

To retain control, the pair should skate as close together as possible. The control comes from the pressure of the pushing hand and arm of the woman against the pulling arm of the man. The backs of both skaters are arched, and their chests are thrown out, with bodies carried erect over the skating blades. No forward bend should come at their waists.

KILLIAN POSITION

In the killian position, the partners both face in the same direction, with the woman on the man's right. Her right hand holds his right hand, which rests on her right hip. The woman's body is placed in front of and against the man's right hip, with her left hand across in front of the man's body, clasping his left hand. The man's left elbow is slightly bent, and his left hand is extended to his left side. His right arm is behind the woman's back, and his right shoulder is behind the woman's left shoulder. A reverse-killian position is performed with the woman on the man's left.

PAIR SPIRALS

Pair spirals are performed exactly like a free-style single spiral except that the partners skate in unison. A spiral is comparable to a ballet arabesque, but the position is held for an extended period of time.

The correct position for a pair spiral has the woman under the man's chest as they execute the maneuver. His right free leg is extended in back, on top of her right free leg, and his arms are over her arms as they are extended to the sides.

You can enter this position from backward right crossovers by stepping forward onto a left, forward outside edge, with both skaters slowly extending their free legs until they reach the spiral position.

WALTZ LIFT

The waltz lift for pair skaters is the same as the freestyle waltz jump, except that the man lifts the woman up into the air and places her down on her back landing edge.

The couple may begin this move from backward crossovers, with the woman trailing slightly behind the man. The man remains backward, and the woman steps forward onto a left forward outside edge (as in a waltz jump), placing her left hand on top of his right shoulder for leverage and her right hand in his left hand. The man's right hand is placed under the woman's left armpit. As she jumps, he applies pressure under her arm, and she assists by pushing and straightening her left arm and simultaneously locking her right arm. In this manner, as in all lifts, the woman creates the leverage that allows the man to lift her into the air. If her arm buckles, the man has no leverage, and the lift will not succeed.

As the woman leaves the ice, her right free leg swings forward to help her rise. At the peak of the jump, her arms and body are locked tightly in the air over his head, as she takes a split position. The woman is then placed slowly and smoothly down onto the ice, skating away on a right back outside edge, in a landing checkout position, with her left arm extended in back and her right hand holding his left. The man should match her checkout position, but should glide forward on his left outside edge, with his right arm and hand extended in back and his left hand holding hers.

LUTZ LIFT

The lutz lift is approached from backward crossovers with the woman in front of the man. The man firmly takes hold of the woman's hips, and the woman holds tightly to the man's wrists. The woman places her right toepick into the ice (as in a lutz jump), and the man lifts her into the air. She assists her partner by pushing down on both wrists and straightening (and locking) her arms and legs. The man lets her go at the peak of the jump, as she is turning in the air. She makes one complete revolution.

The woman lands backwards on the right foot, and the man catches her at the hips, pushing her away from him. She exits on a right backward outside edge, her right hand in his left hand. The man is on his left forward outside edge, matching her position, with his left hand in her right, and his right hand in back. The arms are extended at shoulder height throughout the maneuver.

PAIR SIT SPIN

The couple approaches the pair sit spin from opposite directions on a circle by executing right backward crossovers. They meet at a fixed point, in the center of the circle, by skating a very deep, left forward outside edge. The man remains on the left foot, but the woman immediately switches to the right foot, using it as her spinning foot. The man does a forward sit spin while the woman bends her right knee and extends her left free leg in back of her body. His arms and hands are wrapped around the small of her back, and her arms are up in the air.

To finish the spin, both skaters come into an upright position, with the man finishing on two feet. The woman is still on her right foot as the man pushes her out onto a right backward outside edge. He faces and matches her position while on a left forward outside edge.

LUTZ LIFT . . . as the woman places the right toepick into the ice, she presses down on the man's wrists as he lifts her into the air **(left)**. As the man lets go of her at the peak of her jump, she rotates one revolution in the air leaning backward on the ice **(right)**.

PAIR CAMEL

The approaches for the pair camel are from opposite directions on a circle. Executing backward crossovers, the man and woman meet at a fixed point in the center of the circle. The man swings to the outside of the woman and places his body parallel to hers. His left hand takes her left hand, which is in front, and his right hand touches her right hand, which is in back. The man positions himself so that he is over her— his leg is over her leg, she is under his chest and body. This position is similar to a pair spiral.

Upon completion of the camel, they rise to an upright position and into a matching one-foot spin. Their right free legs are extended in back. The man's left hand is still holding hers, and his right hand has dropped to her right hip for control.

DEATH SPIRAL

If you have progressed this far with pair skating, it is now time to seek professional instruction from a qualified teacher. The death spiral is one of the hardest pair-skating maneuvers and, because of the danger it involves, should not be attempted unless an instructor is present. We will briefly describe the movement

PAIR CAMEL (spinning to the left) ... executed with the man and the woman spinning in the same direction with the man slightly over the woman. The arms and legs are mirrored.

so that you will be able to identify it if you see it performed. The death spiral is approached from right backward crossovers, with the woman trailing behind the man and her right hand in his left hand. As both skaters switch to a right backward outside edge, the man replaces his left hand with his right one, holding tightly onto the woman's right hand.

The man executes a traveling back-pivot, holding his backward outside edge. From the pressure of the pivot, the woman drops back onto a very deep, right backward outside edge, with her left free leg in front of her body and her head nearing the ice. She continues dropping, still clasping the man's right hand, until her head touches the ice. They maintain this position as long as he can sustain his back pivot. She exits by coming into an upright position, moving the left free leg, which was in front, to a full extension in the rear. Her right hand is still holding the man's right hand as he exits on a left forward outside edge.

9

Ice Dancing

Ice dancing became popular in the late 1800s when the Vienna Skating Club took the Strauss waltz onto the ice. Ice dancing differs from pair skating in its concern with edge control and footwork as related to dance movements. For competitive ice dancing, one must have not only a knowledge of skating, but the ability to combine original dance movements with skating techniques.

Ice dancing is an art: every movement of the body is choreographed to a beat of the music. Judging is subjective and frequently controversial. Proper evaluation of a given dance is difficult, and judges often differ in opinion. To further complicate matters, judging is different in the United States, Canada, and Europe. Consult a current rule book for guidance on the various dance requirements.

Ice dancing consists of three categories: compulsory dance, original set-pattern dance, and free dance.

Many rules govern compulsory dancing and free dancing. All dance patterns are illustrated and described in the *United States Figure Skating Association Rule Book*. As in other sports, rules change over the years as new dances are introduced and old dances are revised. Keep in touch with these changes or you'll find yourself outdated.

A compulsory dance consists of a prescribed sequence of steps on the ice, as required by the rule book. The music used must conform with the rhythm and tempo specified for that particular dance. The patterns for compulsory dance are composed of repetitive sequences constituting either a half or full circuit of the rink. This sequence cannot cross the middle of the ice rink except to meet at both ends.

An original set-pattern dance is a compulsory dance using the skater's own choreography (following the structure of a prescribed compulsory dance). Partners must not separate except to change dance holds. A separation cannot exceed one measure of music.

Free dancing has no required sequence of dance steps, and must consist of nonrepetitive combinations of old and new dance movements. Partners express their own concepts and originality through the dance. Each couple chooses its own music, varying in tempo from slow to fast, with not more than four changes of music throughout the program. The music can be any style: jazz, blues, disco, folk dancing, or ethnic. The only music not allowed is classical ballet music because it is considered to be better suited to pair skating.

A free dance program differs from a pair-skating program with its lifts, jumps, and spins having certain restrictions on the number of revolutions permitted (not more than 1½), the height of the lifts involved (all lifts require the man's hands not to be raised above his waist), and the length of time and distance of the separation of partners from each other (not more than two arm lengths away).

The free dance program must be constructed so that the element of competitive dancing is predominant, not giving the character of pair skating to the program. In ice dancing, the interpretation of every movement of the body is choreographed to every beat of the music. Every beat of the music has a step to correspond to it.

DANCE HOLDS

One of the most popular ice dances is the waltz, with its graceful and rhythmic movements. The secret to learning the waltz is to not rush the moves or precede the beat. Clean turns should be performed with turns executed between the partner's feet. There are a variety of waltzes included in the standard dances.

Waltz Hold

The waltz position is the same for ice dancing as it is for pair skating. The man holds his partner firmly between the shoulder blades. The woman's left hand should rest firmly on a spot a little below the man's right shoulder, with her left elbow resting on his right elbow. The man's left arm and the woman's right arm should be extended to the side and held firmly together for control. Again, as in pair skating, it is important for the couple to skate close together. For more details see Pair Skating, page 57.

Killian Hold

Another popular hold is the killian position. It is the same as that discussed in pair skating.

Foxtrot Hold

The foxtrot position is danced side by side with both partners facing forward and skating in the same direction. The man's right hip is next to the woman's left hip. The man's right hand is placed on the woman's left shoulder blade, and the woman's left hand is placed on the man's right shoulder. Both partners should try to skate close together. To achieve this, the man and the woman should press their outside shoulders—the man's left shoulder and the woman's right shoulder—as far forward as possible.

Tango Hold

The partners face in opposite directions with one skating forward and one skating backward. Their hips touch—the woman's right hip is next to the man's left hip. The man is on the right of the woman, and both are perpendicular to the tracing.

The arms are in the same positions as for the waltz, with the man's right hand placed firmly between the woman's shoulder blades and his right elbow raised, but still bent, holding the woman firmly in place. The woman's left hand rests firmly on a spot a little below the man's right shoulder, her right arm resting on his left arm, and her elbow on his elbow. The woman's right hand is in the man's left hand, with both of her arms extended at shoulder height.

PROGRESSIVE STEPS

Progressive steps are a series of three steps on a continuous curve. Step from the left forward outside edge, and place your right free foot on a right inside edge to the side of your left skating foot, no more than half-a-boot-length in front. Return to the original position by placing the left free foot in front of the right skating foot and back to the original, left forward outside edge—outside, inside, outside.

PROGRESSIVE STEPS . . .
facing forward, both the man and the woman skate a left forward outside edge with the free legs matching in back.

The second stage is a right inside edge on the same continuing curve executed together.

The third step of the series consists of stepping back to the original left forward outside edge.

CHASSE . . . facing forward, both partners skate on a left forward outside edge with the right free legs matching in back **(left)**. The weight of both skaters is placed on the right free foot **(right)**, lifting the left skating foot directly up and off the ice with no forward motion. Afterward, the left skating foot returns to the original position next to the right skating foot with the right free legs extended behind.

Backward progressive steps are similar, with the right free foot remaining on the inside of the tracing and to the front of the pushing foot. All steps can be executed in the opposite direction, as well.

CHASSE

The chasse is a series of three steps, starting on your left skating foot, on a forward outside edge. Place the right free foot onto a forward inside edge, directly beside your left skating foot, and lift the skating foot straight up off the ice. Return to the original position by placing your left free foot, which has been lifted off the ice, back down onto the left forward outside edge next to the right skating foot. As in the progressive steps, the chasse is skated on outside, and then inside, and then outside edges.

The difference between progressive steps and the chasse is the upward lift of the second step, or left free leg, with no forward motion of the free foot. Progressive steps move forward approximately half-a-boot-length.

DUTCH ROLLS OR CROSS ROLLS

Dutch rolls can be performed with either a forward or backward movement. For a forward Dutch roll, skate from the left forward outside edge to the outside edge of the right foot. The right free foot is passed around in front of the toe of the left skating foot and placed onto a right forward outside edge with a push from the outside edge of the blade. Little half-circles are made from outside left to outside right, and back again.

For forward Dutch rolls, the opposite shoulder and arm of the foot you are stepping down on leads. The shoulders are in a neutral position.

Backward Dutch rolls are performed much the same way. If you are stepping on the left leg, the right arm and shoulder lead. However, the free foot crosses behind the skating foot before you transfer your weight onto the new outside edge. You are balanced on the ball of each foot with both knees bent. If the knees are straight, the weight will rock to the heel and a fall will result.

CROSS CHASSE . . . the couple executes a left forward edge with right free legs extended in back.

The right free leg has executed a forward crossover onto a right forward inside edge with the back free leg lifted to the outside of the tracing.

The left free leg is placed back onto the ice on a left forward inside edge with the right leg now lifting and extending in front of the tracing.

Skating Routines

Following are routines that vary in degree of difficulty from the more simple, easy-to-perform maneuvers to the complex and more difficult programs.

Start with routine No. 1 and work your way through to the last challenging pattern. Before starting any routine, always warm up by stroking around the ice (both forward and backward), stretching, and doing spirals. Just as the most seasoned competitors and professionals do, start with the basic waltz jump, and as you limber up and get a feel for the ice, gradually progress to your more advanced spins and jumps. All jumps and spins illustrated in the diagrams are entered and exited in the same manner as described earlier in the various paragraphs of the book.

Until you've mastered each routine, don't attempt the next, more advanced program. Unless you've had lots of skating experience, don't be discouraged: each routine will take hours of practice at your own skating level. The routines were designed to challenge your ability. So, good skating!

SIMPLE ROUTINE

1. Begin with dance combination of jazz or a contemporary combination you have made up.

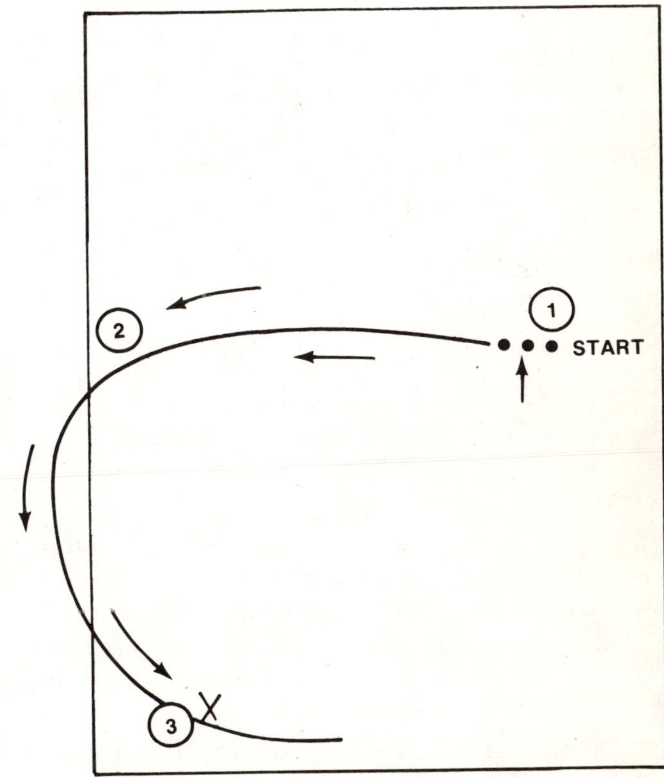

2. Skating forward, execute a left forward lunge with arms over head, or in jazz position of choice.
3. Continue forward, executing a right inside 3-turn into a toe loop jump.

4. Skate toward left side of ice surface and execute left mohawk.
5. After mohawk, skate backward by using back crossovers (right over left).
6. Press a controlled, left back outside edge into a backward spiral.
7. After spiral, bring both feet together and step forward onto the left forward outside edge.

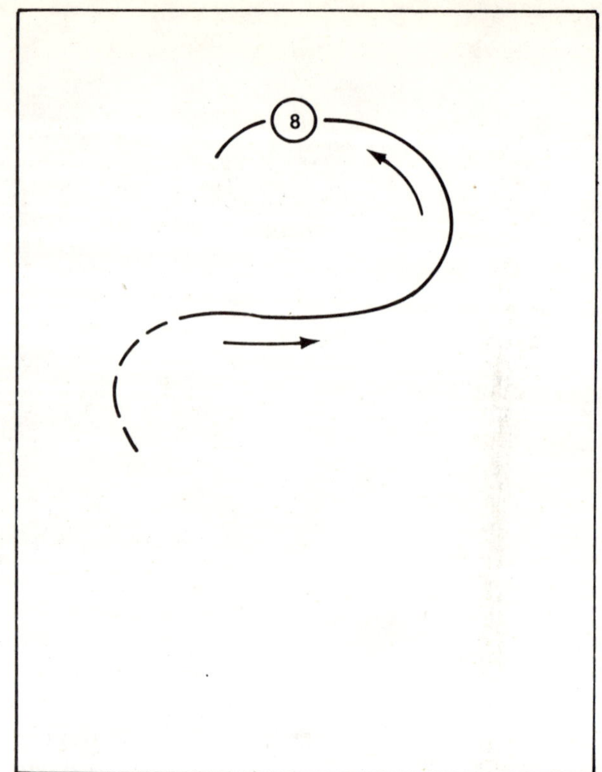

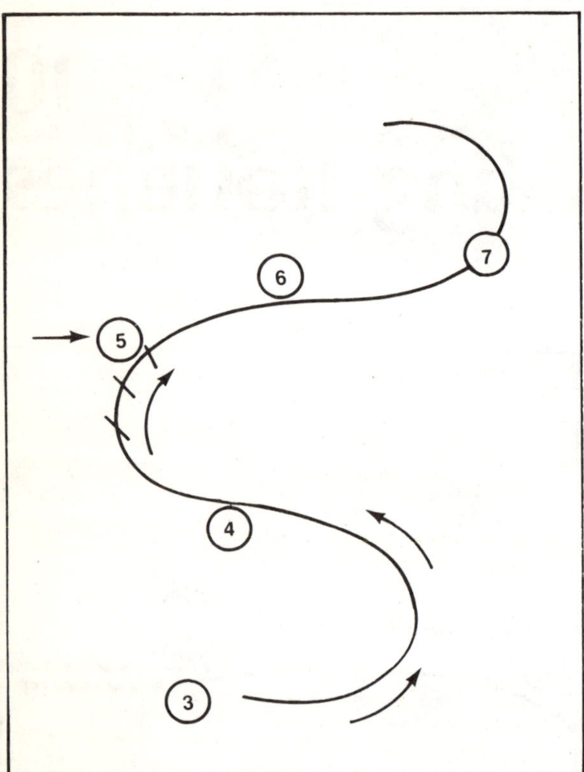

8. Execute loop jump (or salchow if a loop jump is too advanced) around end of ice.
9. After loop jump, skate forward crossovers around curve and execute a left forward outside 3-turn, which brings you across the ice.
10. Skate right backward crossovers (right foot over left) around a small circle in preparation for centering spin.
11. Execute a sit spin, or spin of your choice.
12. Exit from spin by pushing out on a right back outside edge and step forward on the left foot.

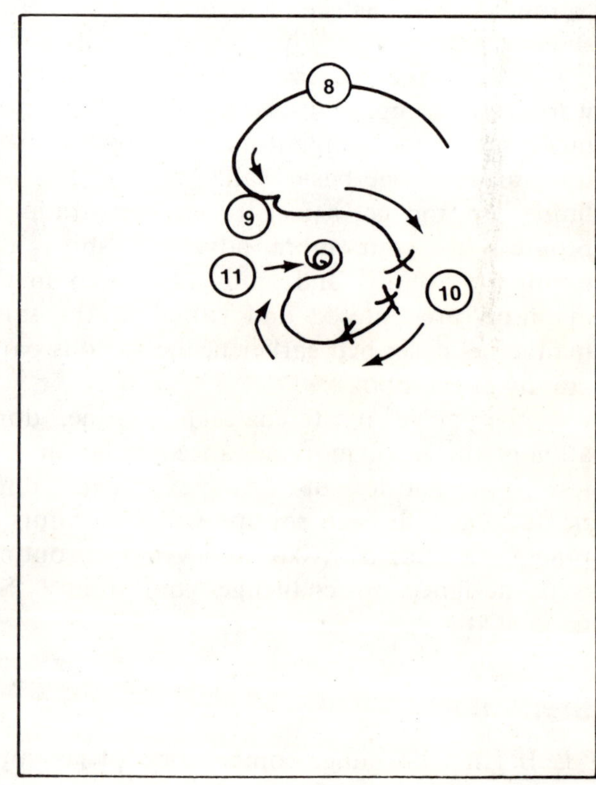

13. Skate forward onto a left forward inside spiral around a large circle in the center of the ice surface.
14. After circle, begin to straighten edge in preparation for flip jump.
15. Prepare and execute flip jump by entering from a left 3-turn.

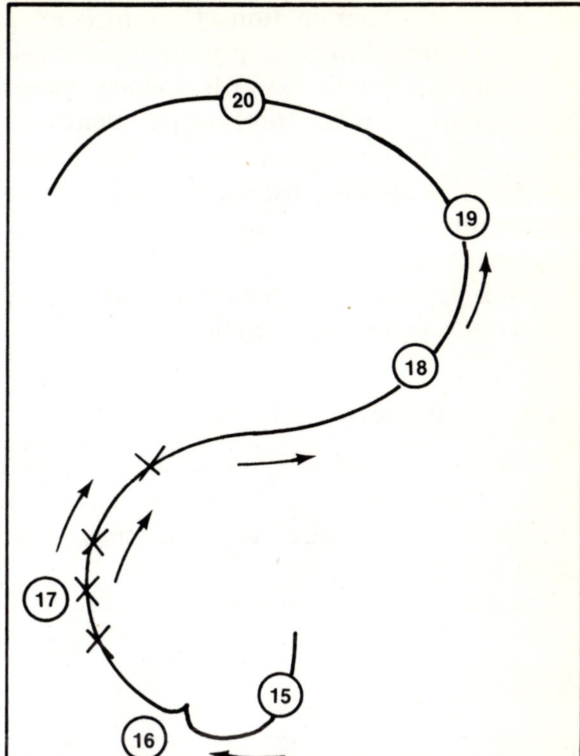

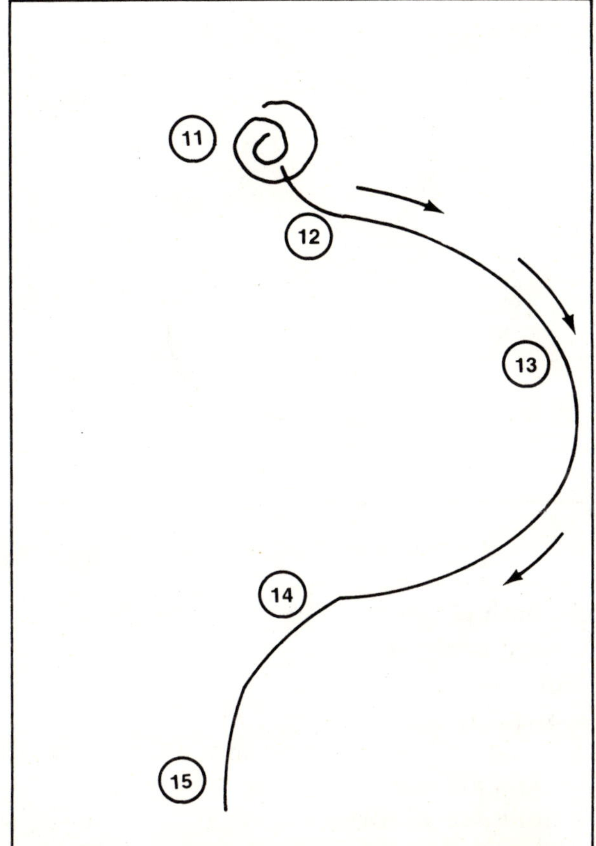

16. After landing of flip jump onto right backward outside edge, step backward onto left backward outside edge and then forward into a right forward outside 3-turn.
17. After 3-turn, skate several back crossovers (right over left).
18. Step forward onto left foot.
19. Execute split jump (rotate to left) by using a right inside mohawk (as described on page 34).
20. Immediately after the first split jump, execute a right mohawk into a second split jump.
21. A third jump, such as a falling leaf jump, flip, or another type of single jump can be

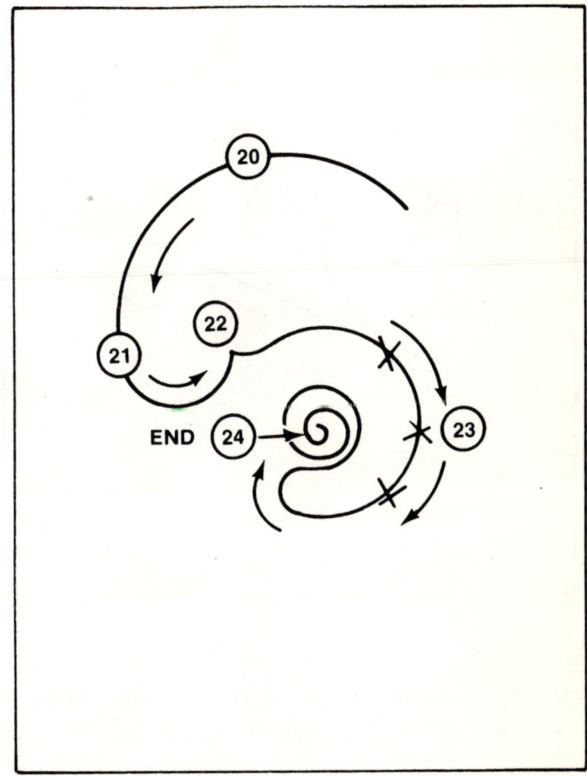

used or a combination of jumps (such as a waltz jump into a loop jump, or a half-loop jump (landing backwards on the back inside edge of the other foot) into a salchow.

22. From the landing of the series of jumps or jump combinations, skate a left outside 3-turn into the center of the ice.
23. Skate backward crossovers (right over left) in preparation for centering your final spin.
24. Center final spin of choice.

ADVANCED ROUTINE "A"

1. Skate a left forward edge on a diagonal in an "attitude" position (as in ballet) or a spiral in a "plea" or bent knee (skating knee) position.
2. Execute a right front T-stop.

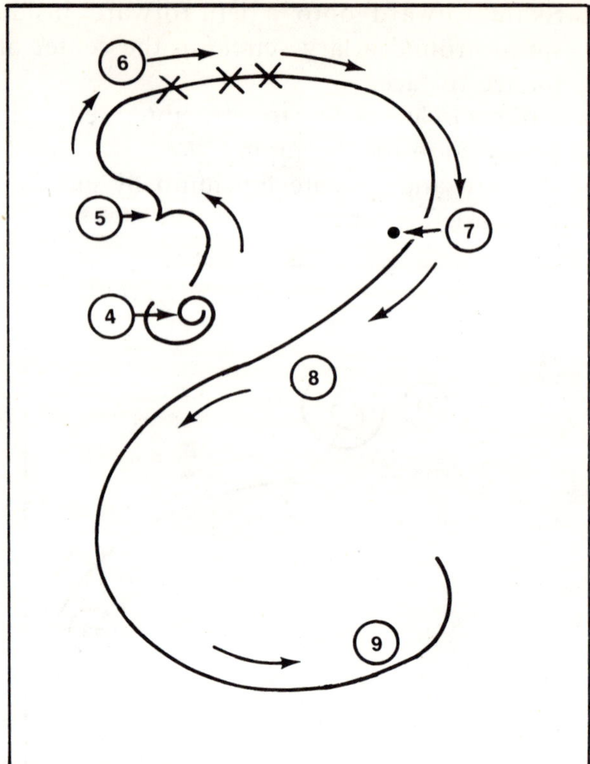

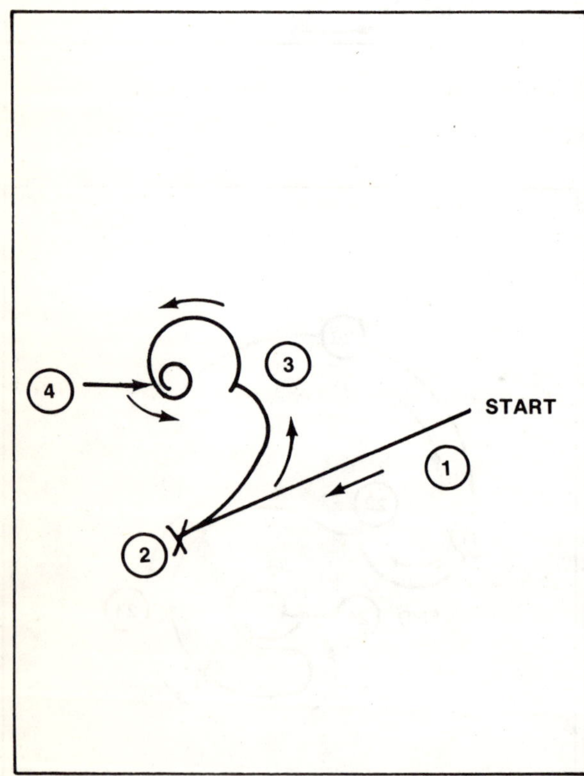

3. Next, turn a forward right inside 3-turn.
4. Execute a back right outside pivot, immediately after the right inside 3-turn.
5. Skate a left forward outside 3-turn.

6. Continue from the 3-turn into right backward crossovers (right over left) around end of rink.
7. Step forward onto left foot.
8. While on left foot push into a long forward spiral around end of rink.
9. Continue with right forward crossovers.
10. Turn a right forward inside mohawk.
11. Skate right backward crossovers (right over left).
12. Step forward onto left foot.
13. Skate a right forward inside mohawk, pushing onto a right backward outside edge.
14. Execute an axel (rotating toward the left).
15. Upon completion of the landing edge, skate a left forward outside 3-turn.
16. Continue into left backward crossovers (left over right) around the end of the rink.
17. After rounding end of the rink step forward onto a diagonal.
18. The diagonal pattern is set up to execute a forward Bauer (left as in diagram, or right if the skater prefers).
19. Continue bauer into sharper, inside bauer, around end of rink.

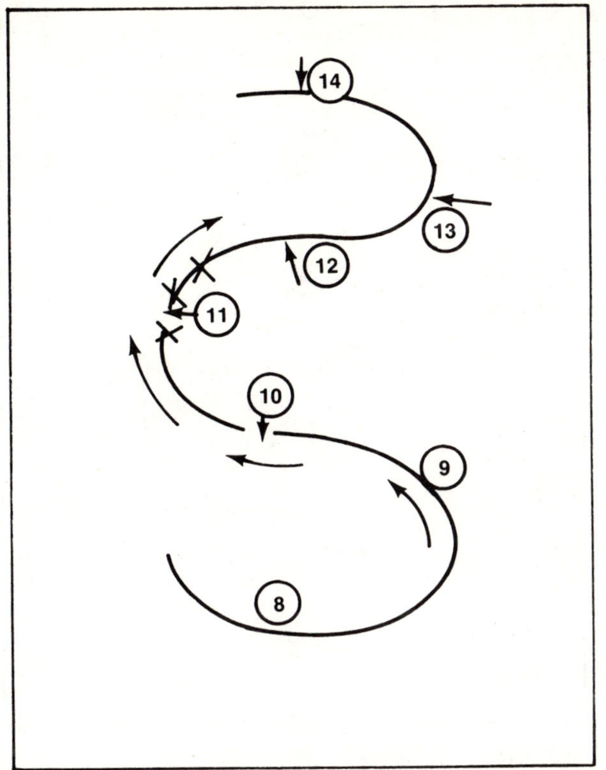

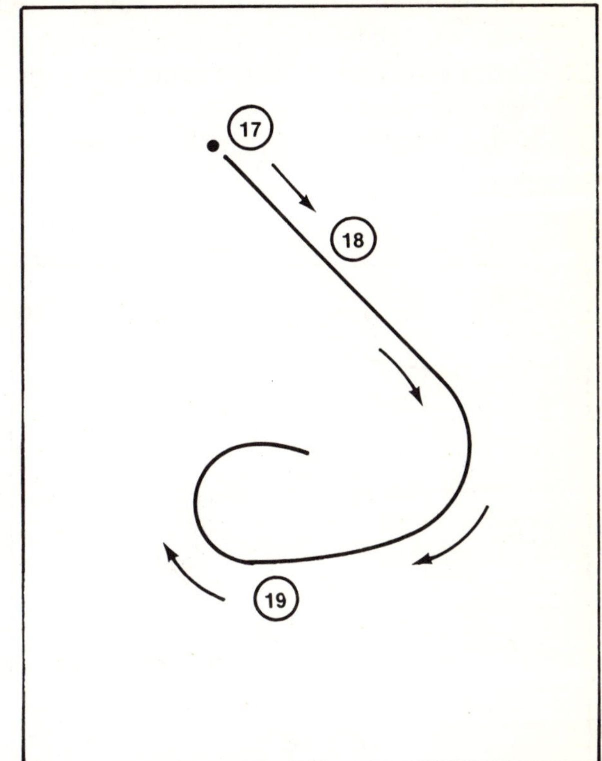

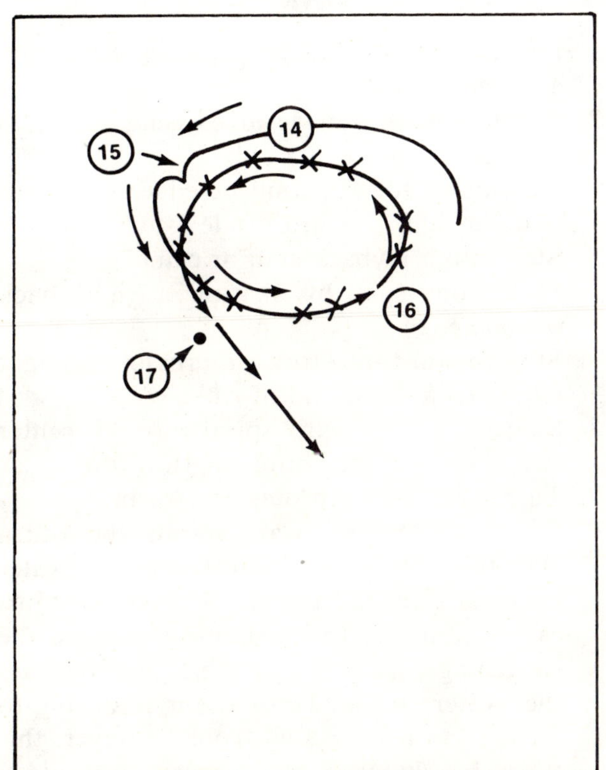

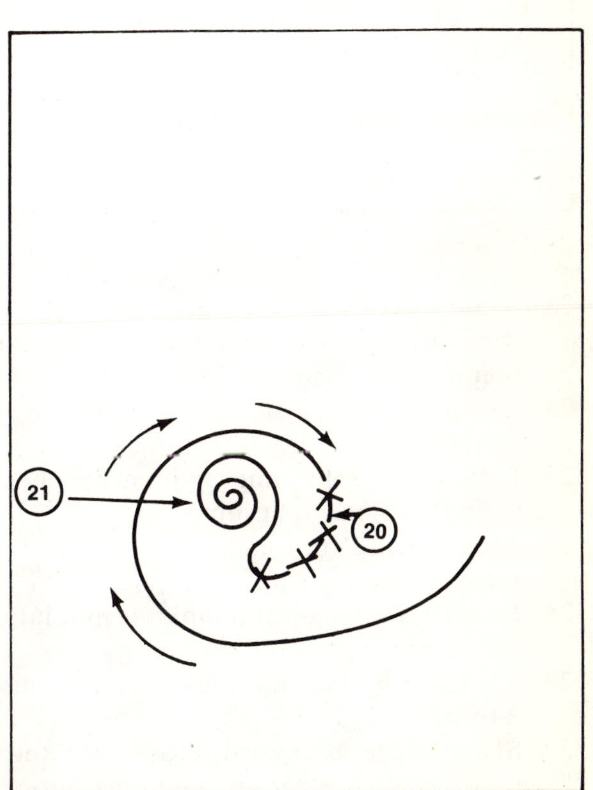

20. Upon completion of bauer, turn backwards, and continue backward crossovers (right over left) "centering" for a sit spin.
21. Execute sit spin or camel spin. Exit spin on right back outside edge.
22. Step forward and turn a left forward outside 3-turn.

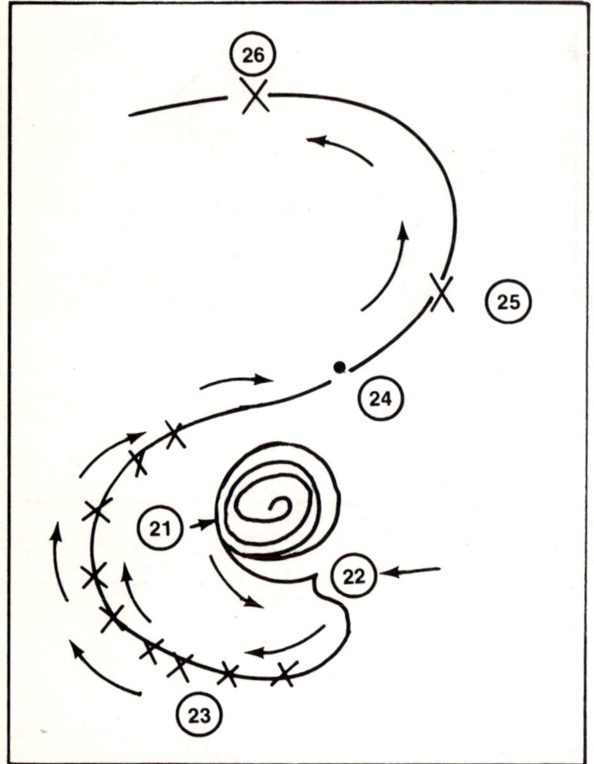

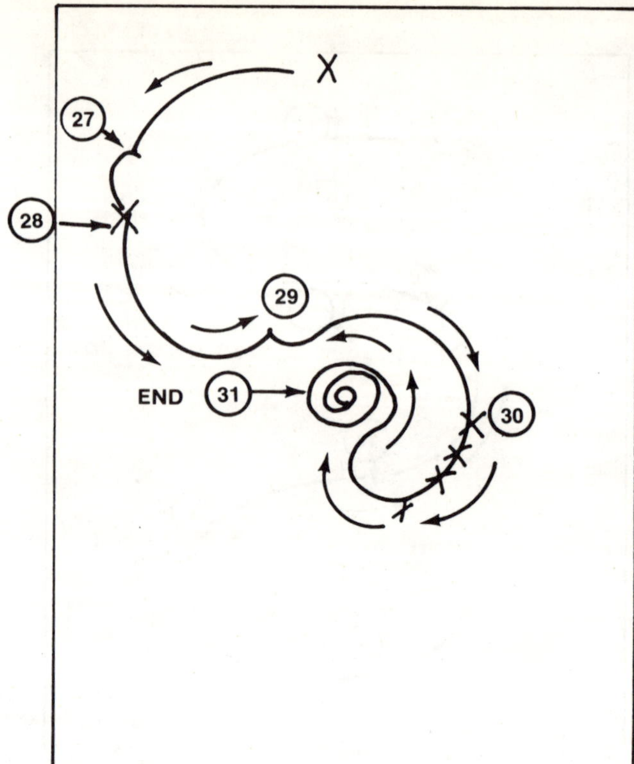

23. Skate a series of right backward crossovers (right over left) around end of ice surface.
24. Step forward onto left foot.
25. Execute a right inside mohawk into a split jump.
26. Follow first split jump by immediately executing a second split jump.
27. Turn a left 3-turn and continue into backward crossovers (left over right).
28. Execute a falling-leaf jump or a split falling-leaf jump.
29. Continue by skating a left forward outside 3-turn.
30. Skate right backward crossovers into a small circle, centering, in preparation for final spin.
31. Final spin of your choice.

ADVANCED ROUTINE "B"

1. Left forward outside edge (using left arm in a ballet move).
2. Right forward outside edge (using right arm in similar movement).
3. Repeat left forward outside edge.
4. Skate a right forward inside 3-turn.
5. Step into a layback spin or camel.
6. Exit from spin by skating a right back outside edge.
7. Step forward into forward crossovers (right over left) around end of rink.
8. Skate a left forward spiral through center straight down the entire length of the ice.
9. Turn a left forward outside 3-turn.
10. Execute a left backward spiral; (the 3-turn and the left back spiral turns the skater backward in the direction he or she just came from) 1st forward spiral is down the ice facing forward, and the 3-turn reverses the skater so that he or she is returning to the direction he skated from, however, this time the skater is backwards, executing a backward spiral in a straight line.
11. Turn a left forward outside 3-turn.

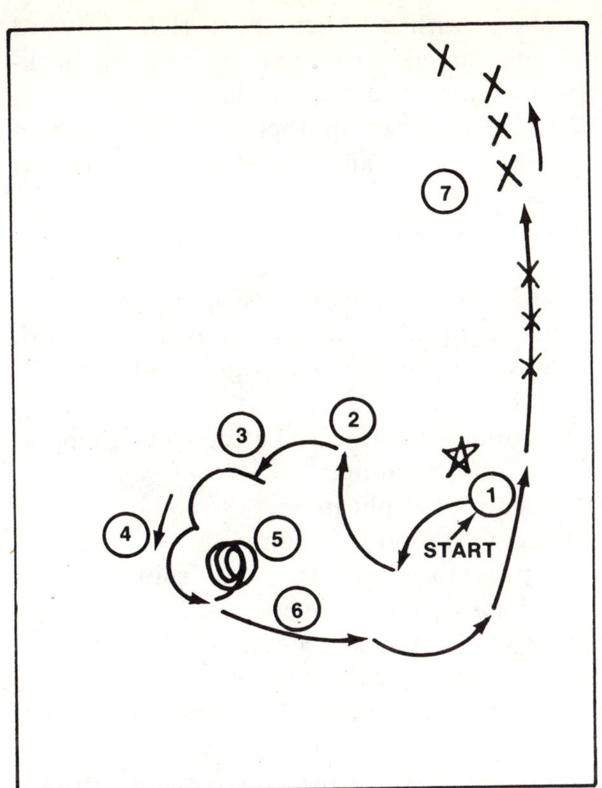
7
3
2
4
5
1
6
START

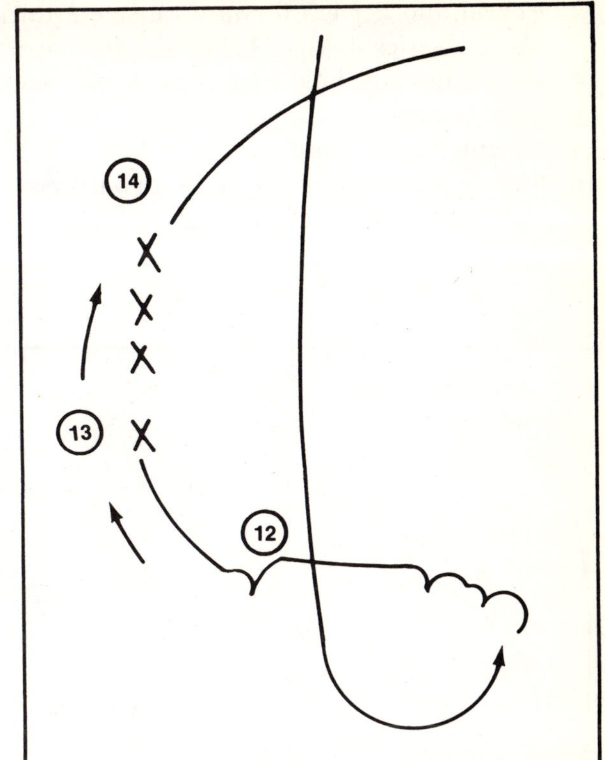
14
13
12

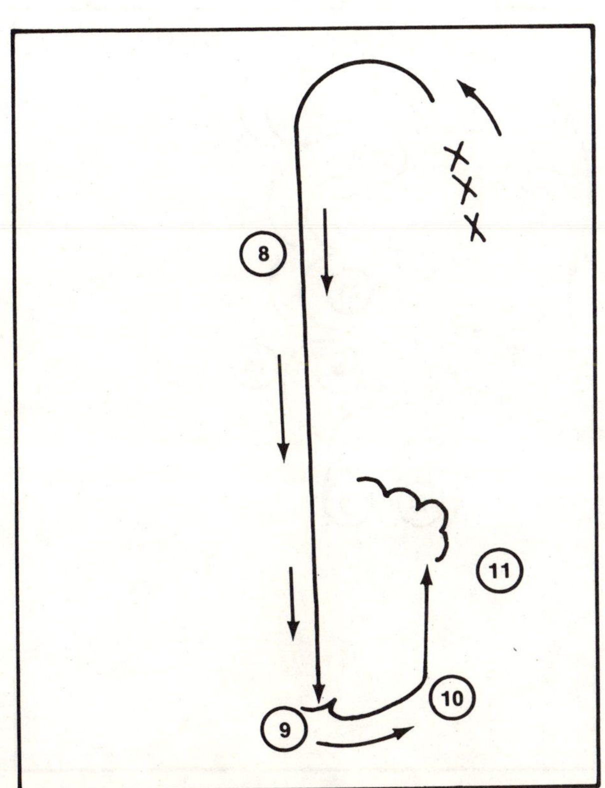
8
11
10
9

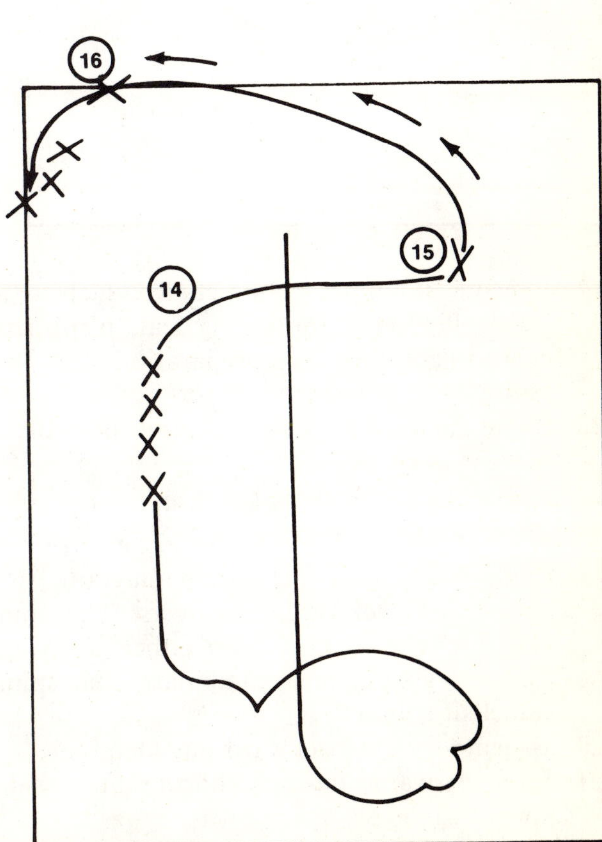
16
14
15

12. Repeat another left forward outside 3-turn.
13. Skate a series of right backward crossovers.
14. While moving, hold and drop into a backward lunge or pose.
15. Execute a lutz jump.
16. Step forward and skate right forward crossovers around end of ice.

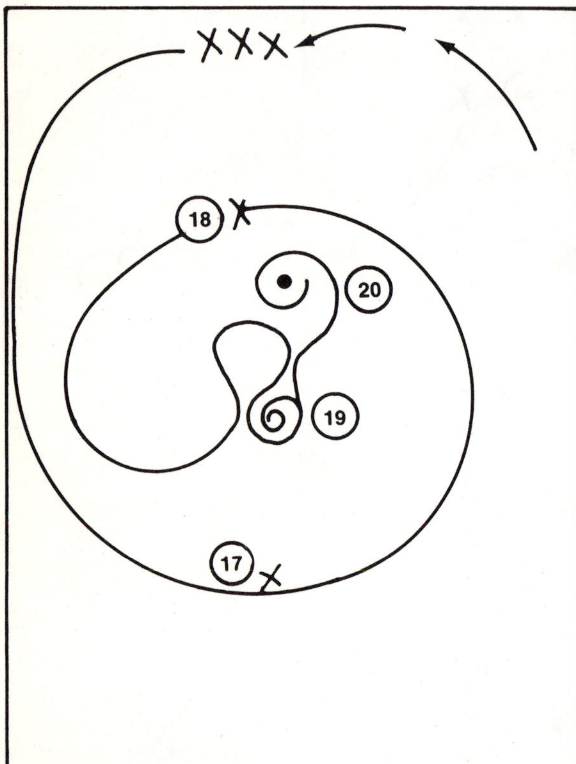

17. Execute a jump of your choice, such as a waltz, flip, loop, or falling leaf, using the correct entrance or preparation for the jump.
18. Skate forward into second jump of choice, such as axel, etc.
19. Upon completion of axel, prepare for spin of your choice by entering either from a right inside 3-turn or (as in diagram) the customary backward crossovers. The spin of your choice could be either a flying camel, layback, or a combination sit spin, camel sit spin, etc.
20. Execute a right backward outside pivot
21. Step forward into a short right inside spread eagle.

22. Follow with another short right forward inside spread eagle. Exit by pushing backward onto left outside edge.
23. Step down onto another backward edge on the right foot and step forward onto left foot.
24. Skate forward crossovers (right over left) around end of rink and execute a left forward outside mohawk (turning toward the outside of the rink) step down backward, crossing over (left over right) and step forward.
25. Continue forward skating in preparation for split jump.
26. Execute first split jump.
27. Execute second split jump.
28. Prepare to center for final spin by skating backward crossovers (right over left) into a small circle and stepping into the center of the circle for the spin of your choice.
29. Stop and face audience and pause (perhaps in a pose). Stretch both arms toward audience. With arms still reaching toward audience, back up on toepicks (taking series of very small steps backwards on toepicks).

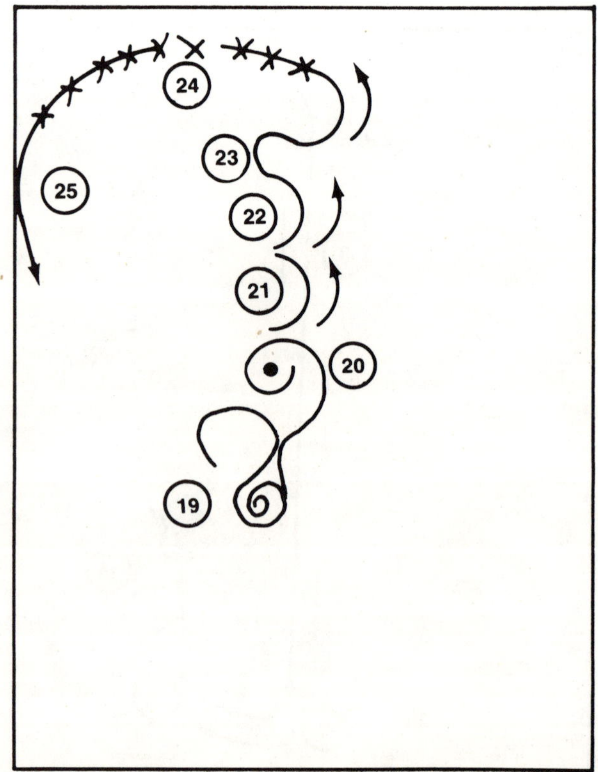

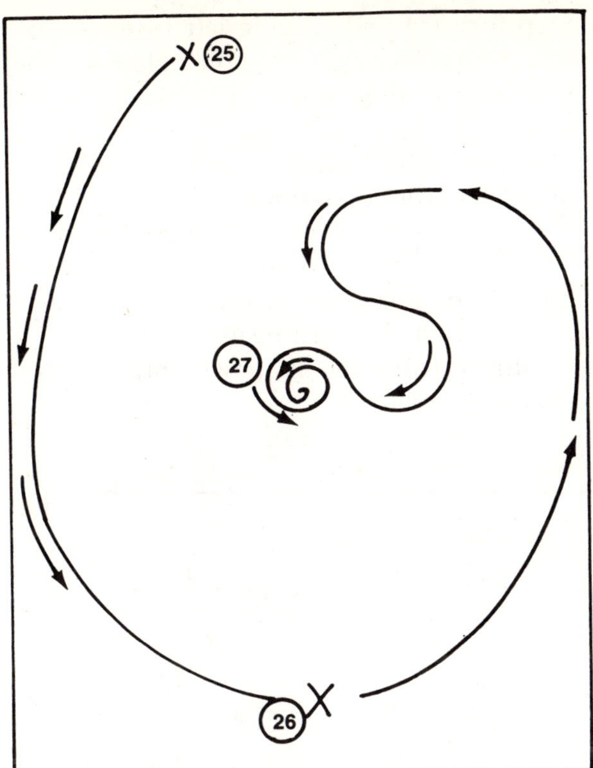

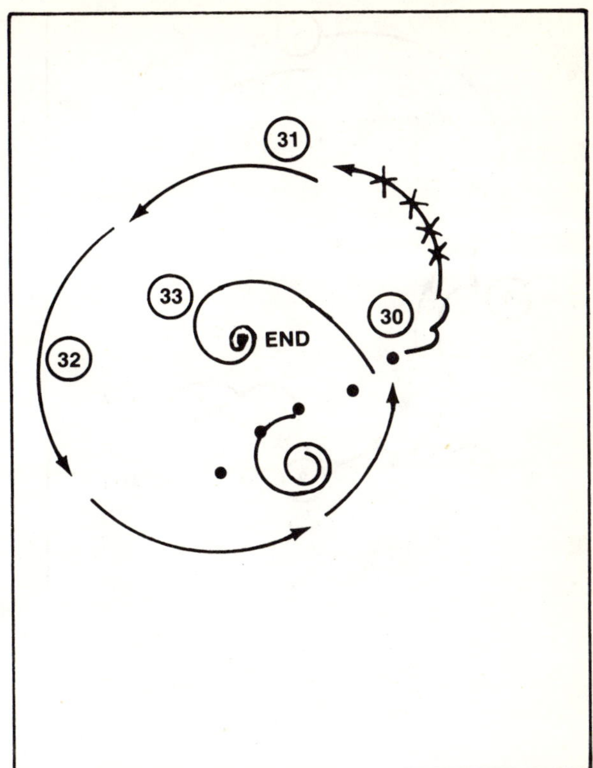

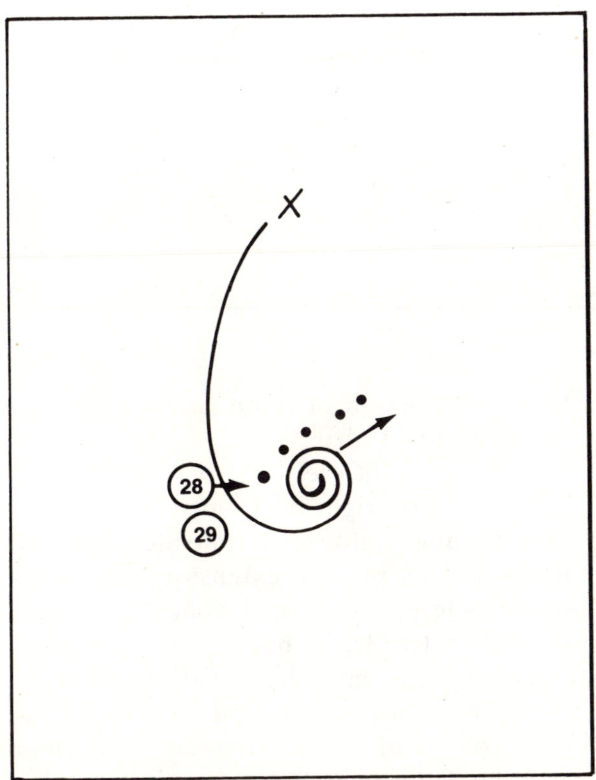

30. Execute a left forward outside 3-turn.
31. Skate forward or as an alternate (and more advanced entrance) prepare for left spread eagle by entering from backward crossovers (left over right).
32. Execute a long forward outside spread eagle, either toward the left (as in the diagram) or if you prefer, to the right; the latter entering from backward crossovers (right over left).
33. Turn a left 3-turn and skate a right backward outside pivot.

Alternate endings:
A.) Back spiral into stop (or final spin).
B.) Back lunge into stop (or final spin).

ALTERNATE COMPLEX ROUTINE

1. Execute a right inside 3-turn and step forward.
2. Skate a left inside 3-turn.
3. Perform any sliding one-foot stop; reach toward audience.

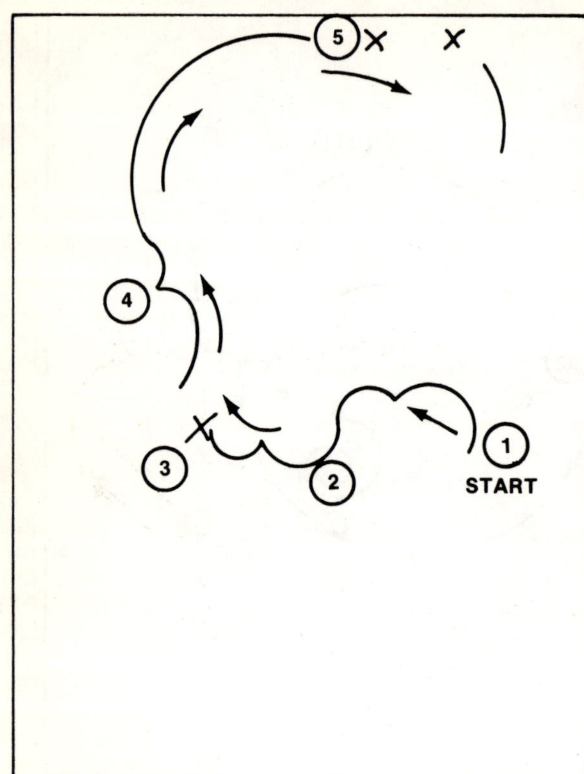

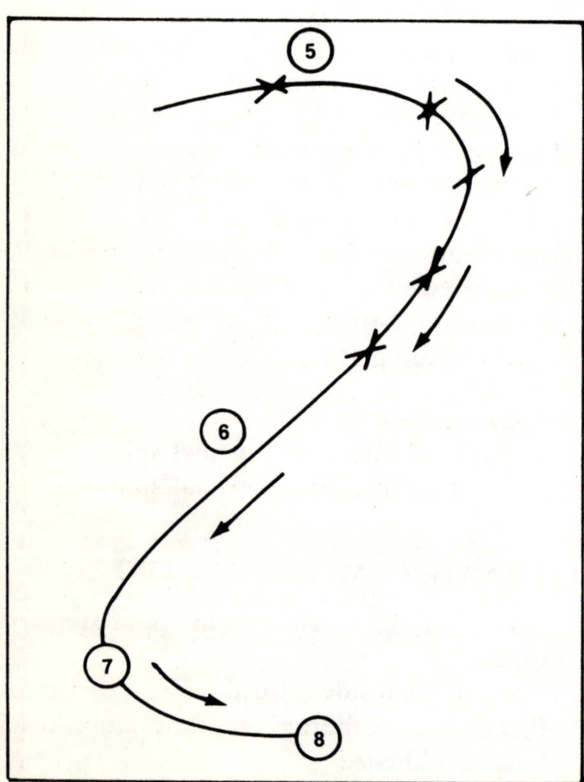

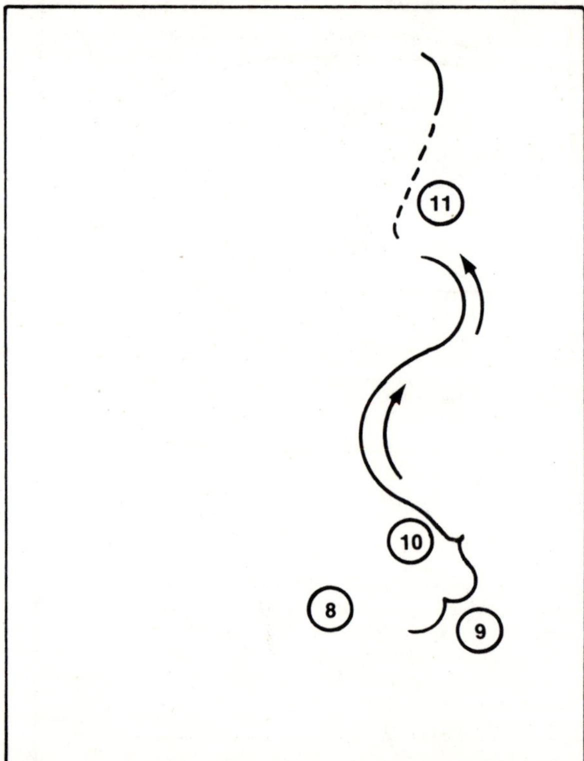

4. Step forward and execute left forward outside 3-turn, stepping wide on right foot and then transferring weight back again to left foot.
5. Continue into backward crossovers (right over left) around end of rink.
6. After crossovers, hold a long back outside edge on the right foot and use arms in a position or some sort of pose.
7. Execute right forward inside mohawk.
8. Continue from the mohawk into an axel (rotating to left).

9. Upon completion of jump, skate a left forward outside 3-turn.
10. Step forward into left forward inside choctaw exiting on right back outside edge.
11. Maintaining right back outside edge, lift free leg (left) into an extension (high kick) or attitude position (see layback spin), ending with a free leg in back.
12. Step forward into combination of waltz jump, half-loop jump, and salchow jump; *i.e.,* from landing of waltz do a half-loop and land backward on left inside edge;

bring right free leg around to front and execute salchow jump.

13. Skate a left forward inside mohawk.

14. Continue into backward crossovers (right over left) into long backward edge on a diagonal (holding a pose).

15. Execute lutz jump.

16. From the landing of the lutz jump continue into backward crossovers (right over left) and prepare to center for spin of choice.

17. Execute spin.

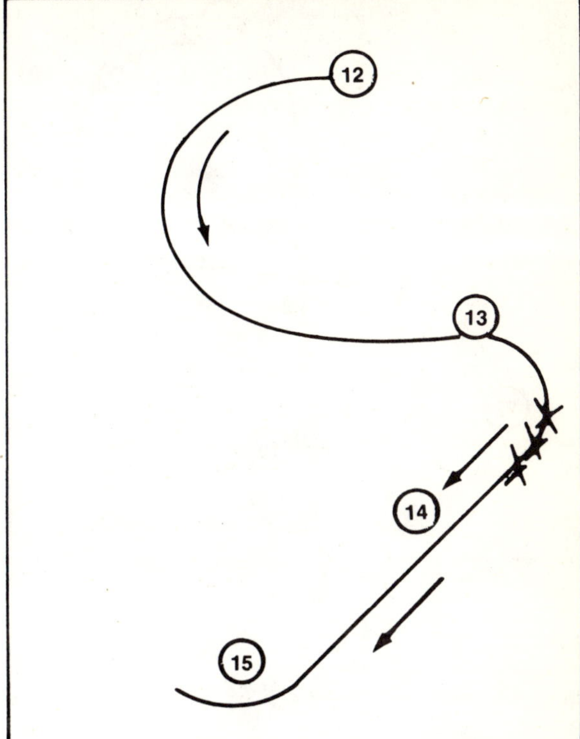

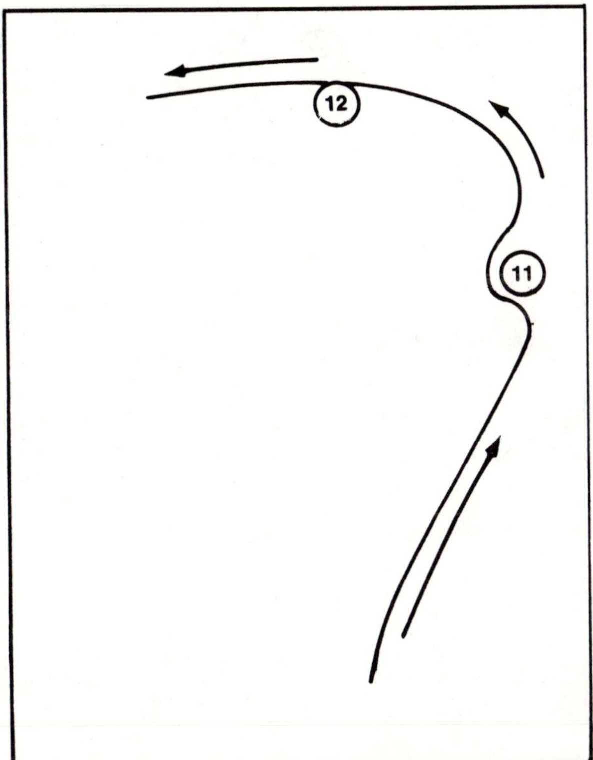

18. Skate a "strut" or rhythmic step up center of ice, "playing to audience."

19. Skate a right forward outside 3-turn.

20. Continue by skating backward crossovers (right over left).

21. Step forward and skate, picking up speed in preparation for split jumps.

22. Execute first split jump (from mohawk preparation).

23. Second split jump (from mohawk preparation).

24. Continue into third jump, such as a falling leaf jump or even another split jump.

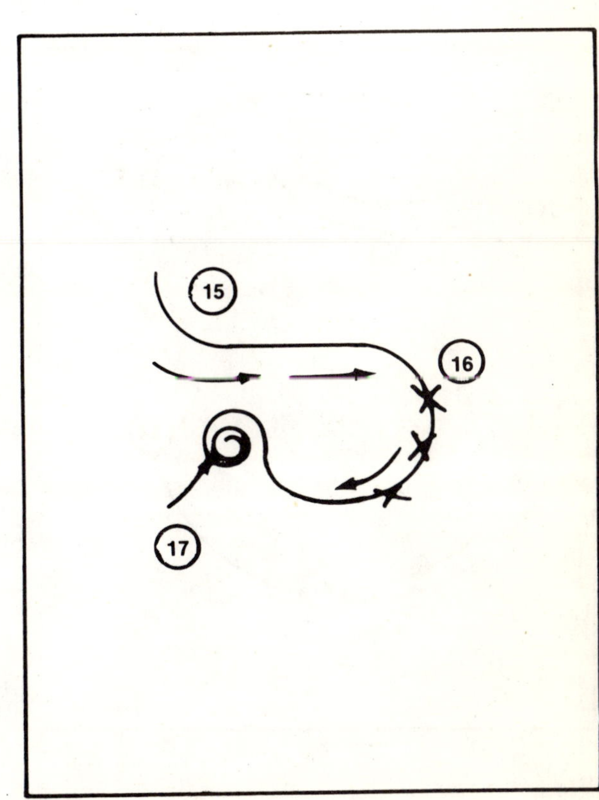

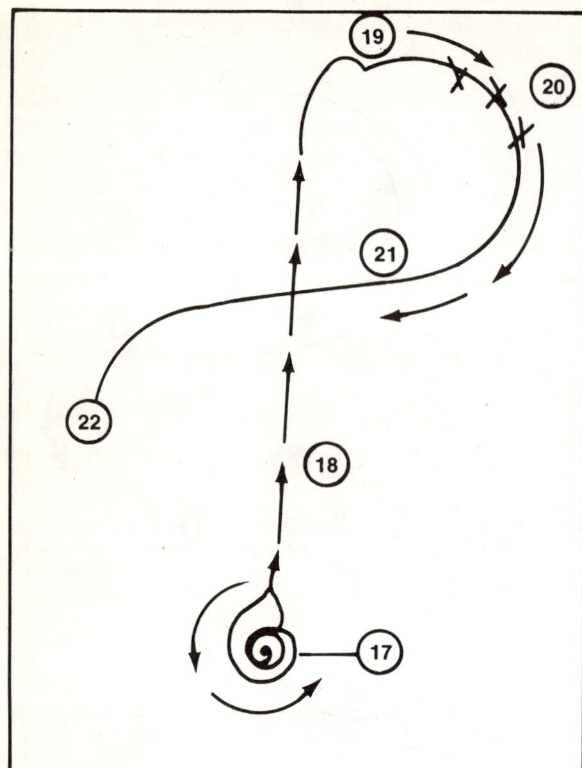

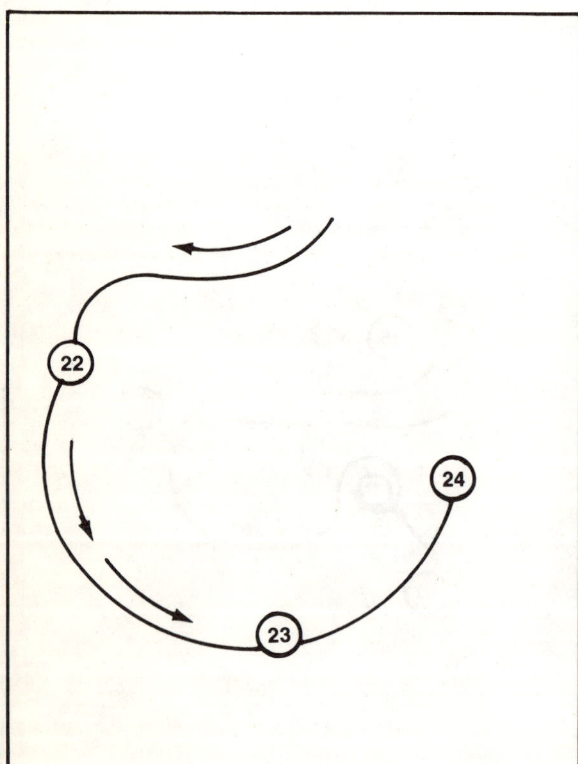

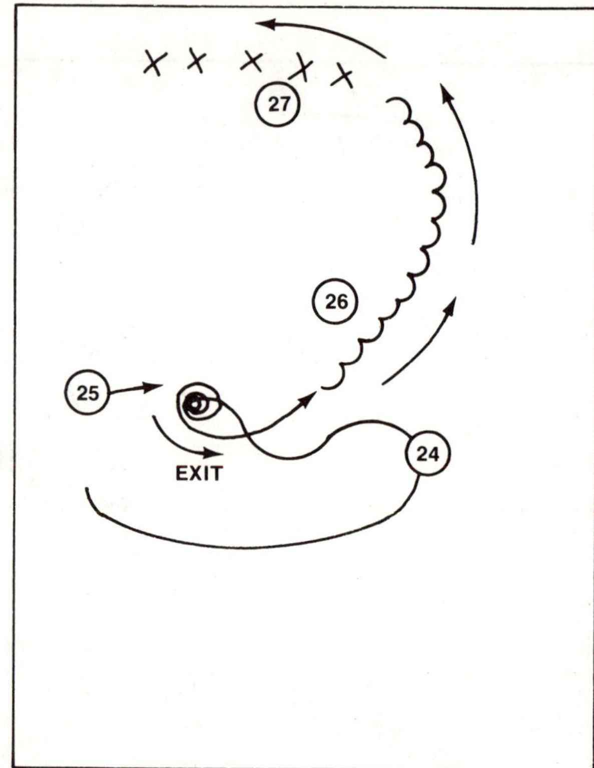

25. After completing the third jump, skate backward crossovers or right inside 3-turn into a "flying camel" (rotating to left) and exit on right back outside edge.
26. Execute a series of traveling toe turns ("chenais turns") to the left.
27. Upon completion of the turns, skate backward crossovers around end of rink (left over right).

28. Upon completion of backward crossovers, step into long forward left (or right) bauer on a diagonal, using entire rink and continuing on inside edge around end of the ice surface.
29. Step forward after bauer and execute a left forward outside 3-turn.
30. Continue into back crossovers (left over right).
31. Try to pick up as much speed as possible and use the backward crossovers to place you into a long, extended back pivot; start-

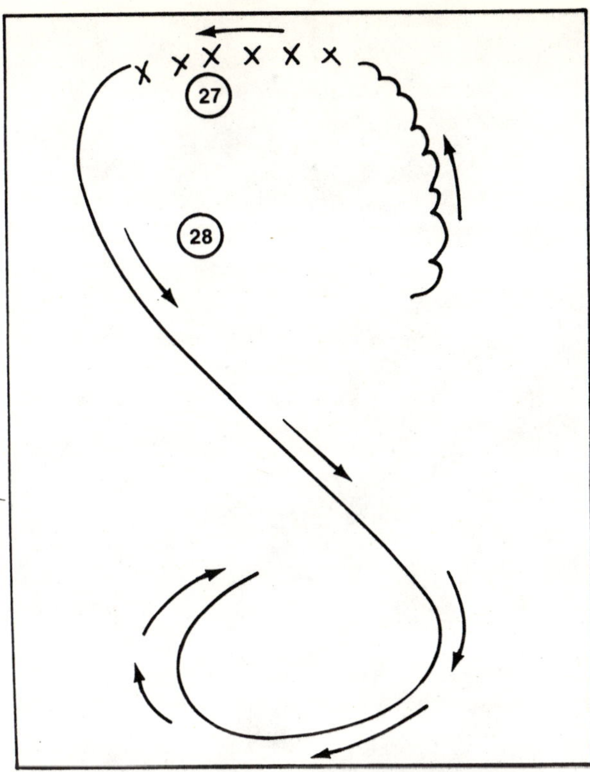

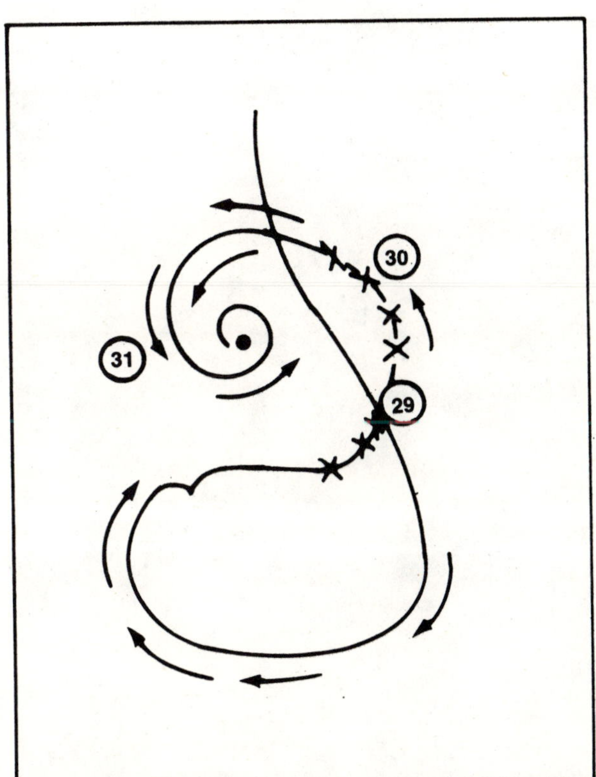

ing in a large circle and slowly winding it into a much smaller, tighter circle.

32. Exit from pivot, by skating two forward right inside 3-turns in succession.

33. Complete the program by either skating a right inside 3-turn or backward crossovers into a final spin, such as a layback.

PHOTOGRAPHY BY
Steve White

11

Advanced Lessons and Professional Training

If skating has become more than just a form of relaxation and fun to you, and your many hours of practice are turning you into a serious skater, then you are ready to find a professional instructor to help you advance your skating career.

But how do you find one, and how do you know that he is right for you? To begin with, call your local skating rink or ask skating friends to recommend someone. Good instructors seem to have a reputation that is well known.

One problem that can arise when taking lessons from any professional is that too often the skater hears from his instructor that the pro's method of teaching is the one and only way to learn skating. Many a skater has made the change from one pro to another only to be told that they have to adjust their method or style of skating to the new pro's way of teaching.

In her lifetime, Ms. Dorsey changed instructors three times, and each time she had to do a slight degree of back-tracking to learn the exact teaching method of her current teacher.

Clarence Hislop of Seattle took her through her National Junior Championship and eighth Test Gold Medal. Then she progressed to Otto Gold of Canada. Mr. Gold was a strict disciplinarian, who required his pupils to adopt his method totally in both compulsory figures and free-skating. After a few years of his tutelage Ms. Dorsey made another change. The traveling distance from Seattle, Washington, where she lived, to the summer training center Mr. Gold held in Kitchner, Ontario, Canada, became too great. Ms. Dorsey then chose her third and final coach to continue her career, with Eddie Scholdan of Colorado Springs, Colorado.

All of her coaches believed that their methods of teaching were the only methods that each skater should follow, which meant that each change brought many weeks of relearning various jumps and spins and other skating maneuvers. It was frustrating for Ms. Dorsey to be allowed to practice only the simple waltz jump when she was well advanced and capable of doing double axels.

All three teachers were excellent, and each

was highly regarded in his field of coaching. Each had different styles and methods of teaching. Yet each method was correct, and each method spawned many champions.

With all the different areas of ice skating today—compulsory figures, freestyle, ice dancing, pair skating, show or group choreography, and competitive choreography—one instructor cannot possibly know each area of skating in depth. It is up to the student to learn what he can from an instructor and then progress to more advanced techniques, even if this means leaving a beloved teacher.

Professionals should be able to share their students with pros who can enrich the students' skating styles in areas outside of the regular pro's teaching abilities. There isn't a professional today who can cover the entire field of ice-skating from compulsory figures to choreography.

Each of today's skating professionals is a product of the teacher or trainer who taught him. And that trainer's style was a product of the teacher who taught him, also. If a skater who has changed pros is doing a maneuver well and cannot, after giving it a sincere try, adopt a new professional's methods of teaching, there is no reason why the skater shouldn't be allowed to continue to use the method that he is familiar with.

Teachers who instill fear into their pupils along with the lessons, and decree that pupils not study with another pro, are only hindering a student's skating ability. A pro needs to be "student-centered" rather than "self-centered." If he is, he will never lack pupils or fear losing a student to another trainer.

For students, always hearing negativism from a teacher or parent can be a dehumanizing factor that tends to develop skaters into "skating machines" instead of expressive, dynamic skaters. Students who have been inspired by

their own self-confidence, motivated by their parents, and encouraged by pros develop all areas of skating and are the ones who shine in the skating rink. You can make a student skate, but you can't make him skate with his emotions—giving just a little more for that perfect performance.

An instructor and a student must form a working relationship that will benefit the student's needs. But it is up to the student to understand his own needs so that he can demand everything he possibly can from his coach. It is this "working together" that will enable a student to progress.

CONCLUSION

Whether you plan to skate for fun or in competition, you can start skating at any age. While serious competitive skaters begin developing their skating abilities at an early age, recreational freestyle skating can be taken up by anyone with the will to learn. Note: Most of Ms. Dorsey's most advanced "recreational" students have gone on to professional shows and several have become principals in major ice shows. You need not be a competitor or a champion to "make it" if you are willing to work.

Ice rinks are becoming more popular, and ice-skating classes are available at a minimal cost. If you are not planning to be a competitive skater, but want to test your skating abilities, you might try taking the standard tests in recreational figure skating, which are provided by the Ice Skating Institute of America (I.S.I.A.), 1000 Skokie Boulevard, Wilmette, Illinois 60091.

You don't have to be a Peggy Fleming or a Dorothy Hamill to enjoy skating. Skating can be as rewarding for a recreational skater as it is for the champion. Your limitations are your own. So, good luck and good skating!